L. B. White

English Sacred Poetry of the Olden Time

L. B. White

English Sacred Poetry of the Olden Time

ISBN/EAN: 9783337777777

Printed in Europe, USA, Canada, Australia, Japan

Cover: Foto ©Thomas Meinert / pixelio.de

More available books at **www.hansebooks.com**

ENGLISH
SACRED · POETRY

OF

THE OLDEN TIME.

Collected and Arranged
BY THE REV. L. B. WHITE, M.A.
RECTOR OF ST. MARY ALDERMARY.

LONDON:
THE RELIGIOUS TRACT SOCIETY,
56, PATERNOSTER ROW; 65, ST. PAUL'S CHURCHYARD;
AND 164, PICCADILLY.
1864.

Preface

FEW passages in the writings of Dr. Johnson have been more frequently quoted than that in which he argues that religious subjects are not capable of poetical treatment. He asserts and maintains this paradox with the utmost brilliancy of diction and ingenuity of reasoning. Yet the fallacies which pervade his discussion of the question are obvious; and his arguments have been replied to so often and so completely, that to attempt a new refutation of them would be a work of supererogation. The Greek sophist, arguing against the possibility of motion, was sufficiently answered by one of his hearers rising and walking across the room. This volume of *English Sacred Poetry* may, in like manner, be regarded as an adequate and practical disproof of Johnson's paradox.

The truth is, that all the various faculties of our being find ample scope in the great truths of revelation. The gospel addresses itself, not to one part of our nature only, but to all. For the intellect, it has truths whose heights and depths and lengths and breadths even angelic intelligencies can never fully explore. To the affections, it offers, not cold abstract dogmas, but a living and Divine Person, whom we love because He first loved us. To the stubborn and rebellious will, it speaks with the authority of a master, yet with the tenderness of a Father, constraining it to a cheerful submission to an obedience which is true freedom. Nor are the fancy and imagination overlooked as beyond its influence. Here the poet may find his grandest or his sweetest themes. The majesty or the grace of God kindled into rapture the souls of psalmists and prophets. "The innumerable company of angels" and "the spirits of just men made perfect" unite in ceaseless praises before the throne. And the church on earth delights to celebrate the Redeemer's glories "in psalms, and hymns, and spiritual songs." Never does poetry better attain its true dignity than when it aspires to lay its choicest garlands at the feet of Him for whom earth had no crown save one of thorns.

So far, then, from poetry being excluded from the service of religion, we should rather say that here "the gift and faculty divine" finds its most fitting sphere and its noblest exercise. The words of Milton are as true as they are eloquent, when he declares the proper office of the poet to be, "to celebrate in glorious and lofty hymns the throne and equipage of God's almightiness; and what He works, and what He suffers to be wrought with high providence in His church; to sing victorious agonies of saints and martyrs, the deeds and triumphs of just and pious nations doing valiantly, through faith, against Christ's enemies, to deplore the general relapses of kingdoms and states from justice and God's true worship. Lastly, whatsoever in religion is holy and sublime; in virtue, amiable or grave . . . . all these things to paint out and describe, teaching over the whole book of sanctity and virtue, through all the instances of example, with such delight to those especially of soft and delicious temper, who will not so much as look upon truth herself unless they see her elegantly dressed,—that whereas the paths of honesty and good life appear now to be rugged and difficult, though they be indeed easy and pleasant, they will then appear, to all men easy and pleasant, though they were rugged and difficult indeed."

Equally groundless was Cowper's expression of regret that our Sacred Poets have been so few. He says—

> " Pity Religion has so seldom found
> A faithful guide into poetic ground !
> Flowers would spring where'er she deigned to stray,
> And every muse attend her on the way."

The following pages will show that our religious poets have been neither few nor faithless. And the diversity of their gifts and callings is even more remarkable than their number. Their ranks are swelled from every walk of life. The soldier, the sailor, the statesman, the lawyer, the physician, as well as the divine, are found joining in the sacred anthem. Sir Philip Sidney, "the flower of chivalry," and Sir Walter Raleigh, the comrade and rival of Drake and Frobisher in their most daring exploits; Wotton, busy in the affairs of his embassy, Vaughan, retreating from the turmoil of the city to practise medicine amongst the mountains of Wales, and Herbert meditating in the seclusion of his Wiltshire parsonage; Milton, the Iconoclast, and Donne clinging to the forms and usages of the past; Bunyan, begrimed by the labours of the smithy, and Waller, with his polished and courtly grace; Baxter, the chaplain to a regiment of Roundheads, and Drummond dying of a broken heart at the death of the King; the Nonconformist Flavel, and the nonjuring Ken—all meet around the Cross as their common centre, their strifes and discords for ever hushed and laid to rest. Christ, who came that He "should gather together in one the children of God, who were scattered abroad," forms the central Sun towards whom they all tend, around whom they all revolve, whilst they shine with a lustre which they borrow in common from Him.

It may be objected, that some of the men whose poems have a place in this Collection failed to exemplify in their lives that devotion which their verses express. But this fact only presents, in a new light, the attractions of the Cross, which can thus compel the homage of its foes as well as the willing service of its friends. Even where the will remains unsubdued, and the heart untouched, the imagination may yet glow and dilate upon the glorious themes which the gospel unfolds,—as Balaam reluctantly celebrated, in strains of loftiest eloquence the glories of God's chosen people, though he himself was to perish at their hands.

Little needs to be said as to the principles on which these Selections from the *Sacred Poetry of the Olden Time* are made. Most of the passages are placed here for their intrinsic merit. Their insertion requires neither explanation nor apology. The presence of a few, however, is due rather to the position and character of the writer than to the value of his poetry. A volume which aims to illustrate the religious literature of two centuries by means of extracts from its poetry, cannot consist exclusively of gems—as well might we attempt to delineate the physical aspects of a country by depicting only its highlands, leaving unnoticed its valleys and plains.

Many of the books from which the following extracts are taken, were composed with earnest prayer to "the Giver of every good and perfect gift," that He would accompany them with His blessing. Often, in the lapse of years, have these prayers been answered. May new answers be now given, new blessings now vouchsafed to a volume in which many a departed saint, "being dead, yet speaketh!"

CONTENTS.

	Page
PREFACE	iii
GEOFFREY CHAUCER—	
The Country Parson	2
ROBERT HENRYSON—	
The Abbey Walk	5
ANNE ASKEW—	
Ballad composed by her when awaiting Execution	8
WILLIAM HUNNIS—	
Certain short and pithy Prayers unto Jesus Christ our Saviour	11
The Conclusion of his "Complaint of Old Age"	12
THOMAS TUSSER—	
Posies for thine own Bedchamber	14
Of the Omnipotency of God and Debility of Man	15
HUMPHREY GIFFORD—	
The Life of Man	16
A Prayer	17
GEORGE GASCOIGNE—	
"Good Morrow"	18
"Good Night"	21
SIR NICHOLAS BRETON—	
From "The Soul's Harmony"	23
The Soul's Longings	24
Farewell to the World	24
SIR PHILIP SIDNEY—	
Psalm cxxxiii	27
Psalm cxxxix	28
Psalm xcvi	29
EDMUND SPENSER—	
The Red-cross Knight at the House of Holiness	33
The Ministry of Angels	36
Hymn on Heavenly Love	36
Hymn on Heavenly Beauty	41
From "The World's Vanity"	43

GILES FLETCHER—
"After they had sung a Hymn, they went out unto the Mount of Olives" 46
Christ's Ascension 47
PHINEAS FLETCHER—
Allegorical Description of Humility and Faith 50
Version of Psalm cxxx. 53
GEOFFREY WHITNEY—
Emblem x. A Wood-cutter at Work . . 55
Emblem xii. A Mower 56
SIR WALTER RALEIGH—
The Farewell 57
Hymn 60
Lines written the Night before his Execution 60
His Pilgrimage 61
JAMES SHIRLEY—
The Vanity of Earthly Glory . . . 62
SIR JOHN DAVIES—
Man's Ignorance of Himself 64
Man's Greatness and Misery 66
The Soul's true Satisfaction only found in God 67
The Conclusion 68
SIR HENRY WOTTON—
"A Hymn to my God in a Night of my late Sickness" 70
The Character of a Happy Life 71
"Hymn made by Sir Henry Wotton when he was an Ambassador at
Venice in the Time of the Great Sickness there " 72
GEORGE HERBERT—
Divine Worship 77
Sin 79
Peace 80
Grace 82
Paradise 83
The Call 83
The Quip 84
Love 85
Sunday 86
J. DONNE, D.D.—
"Hymn to God, my God, in my Sickness " 90
The Day of Judgment 90
From the Litany 91
JOSEPH HALL, D.D.—
Anthems for the Cathedral of Exeter . . . 93

CONTENTS. xi

	Page
WILLIAM DRUMMOND—	
All is Vanity	96
Hymn	97
Heavenly Jerusalem	97
FRANCIS QUARLES—	
Job xiii. 24	99
Job xiv. 13	101
Psalm lxxiii. 25	104
On Jacob's Pillow	106
The Lord is Pitiful and of tender Mercy	106
Trust in God	107
GEORGE WITHER—	
A Prayer for England	109
Hymn for Sunday	111
A General Invitation to Praise God	112
Hymn at Sun-setting	114
A Hymn for a Widower or a Widow	115
The First Martyr	116
HENRY KING, D.D.—	
Sic Vita	117
My Midnight Meditation	118
The Dirge	118
ROBERT HERRICK—	
Litany to the Holy Spirit	121
The Soul	122
To my Saviour	123
HENRY VAUGHAN—	
Morning	124
Sundays	127
Begging	127
Love and Discipline	128
The Rainbow	129
Peace	130
Departed Friends	130
To the Holy Bible	132
"I have learned in whatsoever state I am therewith to be content"	133
JOHN MILTON—	
Sonnet on the Massacre of the Waldenses	135
On his Blindness	136
Praise in Heaven	136
The Morning Hymn of Adam and Eve	137
The First Sabbath	139

	Page
Ode—At a Solemn Music	141
Samson bewailing his Blindness and Captivity	142

SIR THOMAS BROWNE—
Evening Hymn 145

EDMUND WALLER—
The Love of God—I. In Creation 148
                  II. In Redemption 149
Conclusion of the "Divine Poems" 151

JOHN DRYDEN—
The Holy Scriptures 152

RICHARD BAXTER—
The Covenant and Confidence of Faith 154
A Psalm of Praise 157

JOHN FLAVEL—
God's Husbandry 161
The Growth of Grace 162
"A Field which the Lord hath blessed" 163

JOHN BUNYAN—
Stanzas extracted from his Meditations on "Heaven" 164
The Swallow 166
The Flint in the Water 167
Prison Meditations 167

JEREMY TAYLOR, D.D.—
A Prayer for Charity 171
An Advent Hymn 171
Hymn for Christmas-day 172
The Adoration of the Wise Men 173

ANDREW MARVELL—
The Emigrants 174
A Dialogue between the Resolved Soul and Created Pleasure 176

THOMAS KEN (Bishop of Bath and Wells)—
Christian Courage 181
God's Promises 182
Prayer 182
God is Love 183
The Portrait of a Minister 184
Jesus Present 185
A Sinner Converted 186
God, a Father 188

ILLUSTRATIONS.

	Designed by	Page
PREFACE. Vignette	Noel Humphreys	
PORTRAIT OF CHAUCER	T. D. Scott	1
THE ABBEY WALK.	G. Du Maurier	6

On case I cast on side mine eye,
And saw this written on a wall,
Of what estate, man, that thou be,
Obey, and thank thy God for all.
Robert Henryson.

THE TOWER OF LONDON FROM THE THAMES	J. W. North	7
GETHSEMANE	Percival Skelton	11

O Jesu, quicken Thou my soul,
That it may cleave to Thee;
And for Thy painful passion's sake
Have mercy now on me.
William Huniss.

ANCIENT SHIP IN A STORM	J. W. North	16

In worldly seas thy silly ship is tost,
With waves of woe beset on every side.
Humphrey Gifford.

THE RAINBOW	R. P. Leitch	19

The rainbow bending in the sky,
Bedecked with sundry hues.
George Gascoigne.

SIR PHILIP SIDNEY ON THE FIELD OF ZUTPHEN	C. Green	26

"Thy necessity is yet greater than mine."

PORTRAIT OF SPENSER	T. D. Scott	31

ILLUSTRATIONS.

	Designed by	Page
THE RED CROSS KNIGHT AT THE HOUSE OF HOLINESS	*J. D. Watson*	32

Arrivèd there, the door they find fast locked;
For it was warely watchèd night and day,
For fear of many foes; but when they knocked
The porter opened unto them straightway.
He was an aged sire all hoary gray.
Edmund Spenser.

| THE WISE MEN ENTERING BETHLEHEM | *R. P. Leitch* | 39 |

Whom greatest princes sought on lowest knee.
Edmund Spenser.

| THE LION AND THE WASP | *J. Wolf* | 44 |

A mighty lion, lord of all the wood,
Having his hunger thoroughly satisfied
With prey of beasts and spoil of living blood,
Safe in his dreadless den him sought to hide.
Edmund Spenser.

| HUMILITY AND FAITH | *J. W. North* | 51 |

So lowest dales we let at highest rates;
So creeping strawberries yield daintiest cates,
The Highest highly loves the low, the lofty hates.
Phineas Fletcher.

| SIR WALTER RALEIGH IN THE TOWER | *G. Du Maurier* | 60 |

But from this earth, this grave, this dust,
The Lord shall raise me up, I trust.

| THE STUDENT'S APARTMENT | *C. Green* | 65 |

We that acquaint ourselves with every zone,
And pass both tropics, and behold both poles,
When we come home are to ourselves unknown,
And unacquainted still with our own souls.
Sir John Davis.

VENICE	*Percival Skelton*	73
BEMERTON CHURCH	*J. W. North*	75
SALISBURY FROM THE PATH TO BEMERTON	*Percival Skelton*	76

ILLUSTRATIONS. XV

	Designed by	Page
SUNDAY	J. W. North	86

O day most calm, most bright,
The fruit of this, the next world's bud,
Th' endorsement of supreme delight,
Writ by a Friend, and with His blood.
George Herbert.

OLD ST. PAUL'S	J. W. North	89
INTERIOR OF EXETER CATHEDRAL	Percival Skelton	92
FLEEING FROM WRATH	J. Tenniel	101

'Tis vain to flee; 'tis neither here nor there
Can 'scape that hand, until that hand forbear:
Ah me! where is He not, that's everywhere?
Francis Quarles.

ENGLAND'S BLESSINGS	J. W. North	108

What pleasant groves, what goodly fields!
How fruitful hills and dales have we!
George Wither.

THE DIRGE	Percival Skelton	119

It is a dial—which points out
The sun-set, as it moves about.
Henry King, D.D.

"SERVE GOD BEFORE THE WORLD"	J. D. Watson	125

Yet never sleep the sun up; prayer should
Dawn with the day, there are set, awful hours
'Twixt heaven and us; the manna was not good
After sun-rising, for day sullies flowers.
Rise to prevent the sun; sleep doth sins glut,
And heaven's gate opens when the world's is shut.
Henry Vaughan.

JOHN MILTON AND HIS DAUGHTERS	C. Green	136

"Doth God exact day-labour, light denied?"
I fondly ask: but Patience, to prevent
That murmur, soon replies, "God doth not need
Either man's work, or his own gifts; who best
Bear His mild yoke, they serve Him best."

ILLUSTRATIONS.

	Designed by	Page
WALLER'S TOMB AT BEACONSFIELD	*Percival Skelton*	147
DARTMOUTH	*J. W. North*	160
THE GREEN HOUSE, ELSTOW	*J. W. North*	164
THE EMIGRANTS	*J. D. Watson*	174

    Thus sang they, in the English boat,
    A holy and a cheerful note,
    And all the way, to guide their chime,
    With falling oars they kept the time.
                      Andrew Marvell.

LONGLEAT HOUSE	*J. W. North*	180
THE PORTRAIT OF A MINISTER	*F. Walker*	184

    Give me the priest these graces shall possess,
    Of an ambassador, the just address :
    A father's tenderness, a shepherd's care,
    A leader's courage, which the cross can bear;
    *   *   *   *   *
    A prophet's inspiration from above,
    A teacher's knowledge, and a Saviour's love.
                      Bishop Ken.

The whole of the designs have been executed under the superintendence of Mr. Edward Whymper, by whom they have been engraved.

CHAUCER.

GEOFFREY CHAUCER.

BORN A.D. 1328; DIED A.D. 1400.

GEOFFREY CHAUCER, commonly called the Father of English Poetry, was born in London, probably in 1328, and died in 1400 at the age of seventy-two. His life was as varied as it was long. First a law-student, afterwards a soldier, a prisoner in France, attached to the person of King Edward III. from whom he received a pension, employed at home and abroad in the service of the State, closely connected by domestic ties with the family of John of Gaunt, comptroller of the customs in the port of London, and a member of parliament for the county of Kent, he saw life from every point of view. Thus his poems have a special value, setting before us most vividly the habits of life and modes of thought of the English of his day. Interesting as they are to those who study the history of our country, they are no less so to those who study its literature, both from the freshness and vigour of their descriptions, and from the light which they throw upon the growth of our language. They are the works of him whom Spenser called "a well of English undefiled." But they have an additional interest for English Protestants, as the writings of the contemporary of the great reformer John Wyckliffe; and as bearing witness to the strong feeling which existed in the minds of our countrymen, even at that early date, against the tyranny and the abuses of the Church of Rome. Chaucer has few claims to be considered a sacred poet, and much that he wrote is stained with the coarseness and licence of the age in which he lived; but it has been thought well to give a place in this collection to his well-known description of *The Parson*, which reminds us how the work of a faithful minister of Christ has been the same at all times. Just before his death "in his great anguish" he composed a short poem expressive of deep sorrow for the sins and follies of his life, concluding with these touching words:—

> Here is no home, here is but wilderness,
> Forth, pilgrim! forth, beast, out of thy stall!
> Look up on high and thanké God for all!
> Weivé[1] thy lusts, and let thy ghost[2] thee lead,
> And truth shall thee deliver, it is no dread.

In the following extracts the spelling is slightly modernized. Much of the apparent roughness and inharmoniousness of Chaucer's versification will disappear if it be remembered that the final *e*, which is now always mute, was then commonly sounded.

THE COUNTRY PARSON.

A GOOD man there was of religion,
That was a pooré parson of a town,
But rich he was of holy thought and work;
He was also a learned man, a clerk,
That Christés Gospel truly wouldé preach;
His parishens devoutly would he teach.
Benign he was, and wonder diligent,
And in Adversity full patient,
And such he was y-proved often sithes;[3]
Full loth were he to cursen for his tithes,
But rather would he given, out of doubt,
Unto his pooré parishens about,

---

[1] Waive, forsake.   [2] Spirit.   [3] Times.

Of his offering and eke of his substánce;
He could in little thing have suffisance.
Wide was his parish, and housen far asunder,
But he ne left nought, for no rain nor thunder,
In sickness, and in mischief, to visit
The furthest in his parish, moche and light,[1]
Upon his feet, and in his hand a staff.
This noble example to his sheep he gave,
That first he wrought, and after that he taught.
Out of the Gospel he the wordés caught,
And this figúre he added yet thereto,
That if gold rusté what should iron do?
And if a priest be foul, on whom we trust,
No wonder is a lewed-man[2] to rust.
And shame it is, if that a priest take keep,
To see a fouled shepherd, and clean sheep.
Well ought a priest, example for to give
By his cleanness, how that his sheep should live.

He setté not his benefice to hire,
And left his sheep encumbered in the mire,
And ran unto London, to Saint Poules,
To seeken him a chaunterie for souls,
Or with a brotherhood to be withhold;[3]
But dwelt at home, and kepté well his fold,
So that the wolf ne made it not miscarry.
He was a shepherd, and no mercenary.
And though he holy were and virtuous,
He was to sinful men not despitous,

---

[1] Great and small.   [2] Layman.
[3] Or be kept from his duties with a brotherhood of monks.

Ne of his speeché dangerous ne digne,[1]
But in his teaching discreet and benign.
To drawen folk to heaven by fairness,
By good example, was his business.
But if were any person obstinate,
What so he were of low or high estate,
Him would he snibben[2] sharply for the nones.[3]
A better priest I trow, that no where none is,
He waited after no pomp nor reverence,
Nor maked him a spicéd conscience;
But Christés lore, and his Apostles twelve
He taught, but first he followed it himself.

---

[1] Threatening or disdainful.   [2] Snub, reprove.   [3] For that occasion, once for all.

ROBERT HENRYSON.

DIED A.D. 1500.

ALL that is known of this Scotch poet is that he was a Benedictine monk, and subsequently became schoolmaster of Dunfermline. His productions were numerous, consisting of a volume of fables, the "Testament of Fair Cressid," and some miscellaneous pieces. He died at a good old age, about the year 1500.

THE ABBEY WALK.

"I have learned, in whatsoever state I am, therewith to be content."
Phil. iv. 11.

ALONE as I went up and down
  In an abbey was fair to see,
Thinking what consolation
  Was best into adversity,
On case[1] I cast on side mine eye,
  And saw this written on a wall,
Of what estate, man, that thou be,
  Obey, and thank thy God for all.

Thy kingdom, and thy great empire,
  Thy royalty, nor rich array,
Shall nought endure at thy desire,
  But, as the wind, will wend away.

[1] By chance.

Thy gold, and all thy goodes gay,
    When fortune list, will from thee fall;
Since thou such samples see'st each day,
    Obey, and thank thy God for all.

Though thou be blind, or have an halt,
    Or in thy face deformed ill,
So it come not through thy default,
    No man should thee reprove by skill.[1]
Blame not thy Lord, so is his will:
    Spurn not thy foot against the wall,
But with meek heart and prayer still,
    Obey, and thank thy God for all.

God, of his justice, must correct,
    And of his mercy, pity have:
He is a Judge, to none suspect,
    To punish sinful man and save.
Though thou be lord above the laif,[2]
    And afterward made bound and thrall,
A poor beggar with scrip and staiff,
    Obey, and thank thy God for all.

In wealth be meek, heich[3] not thyself,
    Be glad in wilful poverty;
Thy power, and thy worldly pelf,
    Is nought but very vanity:
Remember Him that died on tree,
    For thy sake tasted bitter gall;
Who heis[4] low hearts and lowers high;
    Obey, and thank thy God for all.

---

[1] By right.   [2] The rest.   [3] Lift up.   [4] Exalts.

THE ABBEY WALK.

THE TOWER OF LONDON.

ANNE ASKEW.

BORN A.D. 1520; DIED A.D. 1546.

ANNE ASKEW was one of the numerous victims of persecution in the days of Henry VIII. She was the daughter of Sir William Askew, a gentleman of good family and property in Lincolnshire. She herself corresponded with Queen Catherine Parr, and was on friendly terms with many of the ladies of the court. Having embraced the Protestant faith, she was turned out of doors by her husband, Mr. Kyme. In March, 1545, she was arrested on a charge of heresy, thrown into prison, and most cruelly tortured. When Sir Anthony Knevett, the constable of the Tower, and the jailor, refused to continue the torture longer, Wriothesley, the chancellor, and Rich, applied the rack with their own hands. "And so, quietly and patiently praying unto the Lord, she abode their tyranny, till her bones and joints were almost plucked asunder." Having displayed wonderful firmness, readiness, and scriptural knowledge in the various examinations which she underwent, she was burned at Smithfield, July 16, 1546. Much of her time in prison was spent in writing, and many of her compositions display rare abilities. One of them is prefaced by these striking words: *Written by me, Anne Askew, that neither desire death, nor yet fear his might; and as merry as one bound to heaven.* The following ballad was composed by her when awaiting execution.

 Like as the armèd knight
  Appointed to the field,
 With this world will I fight,
  And faith shall be my shield.

 Faith is that weapon strong
  Which will not fail at need;
 My foes therefore among,
  Therewith will I proceed.

 As it is had in strength
  And force of Christe's way,
 It will prevail at length
  Though all the devils say nay.

 Faith in the Fathers old
  Obtained righteousness,
 Which makes me very bold
  To fear no world's distress.

I now rejoice in heart,
  And hope bids me do so;
For Christ will take my part,
  And ease me of my woe.

Thou say'st, Lord, whoso knock
  To them wilt Thou attend;
Undo therefore the lock
  And Thy strong power send.

More enemies now I have
  Than hairs upon my head,
Let them not me deprave,
  But fight Thou in my stead.

On Thee my care I cast;
  For all their cruel spite,
I set not by their haste,
  For Thou art my delight.

I am not she that list
  My anchor to let fall
For every drizzling mist:
  My ship's substantial.

Not oft use I to write
  In prose, nor yet in rhyme;
Yet will I show one sight
  That I saw in my time.

I saw a royal throne
  Where Justice should have sat,
But in her stead was one
  Of moody cruel wit.

Absorbed was righteousness
  As by the raging flood,
Satan in his excess
  Suck'd up the guiltless blood.

Then thought I,—Jesus, Lord,
  When Thou shalt judge us all,
Hard is it to record
  On these men what will fall.

Yet, Lord, I Thee desire
  For that they do to me,
Let them not taste the hire
  Of their iniquity.

GETHSEMANE.

WILLIAM HUNISS,

ONE of the Gentlemen of the Chapel Royal under Edward VI. and Elizabeth, and also Master of the Chapel Boys. His principal productions were a metrical version of the book of Genesis, which he entitled *A Hive full of Honey*, and a volume of Psalms and Hymns called *A Handful of Honeysuckles*.

"CERTAIN SHORT AND PITHY PRAYERS UNTO JESUS CHRIST OUR SAVIOUR."

I.

O JESU sweet, grant that Thy grace
   Always so work in me,
I may desire the thing to do
   Most pleasing unto Thee.

O Jesu meek, Thy will be mine,
  My will be Thine also;
And that my will may follow Thine
  In pleasure, pain, and woe.

O Jesu, what is good for me
  Is aye best known to Thee;
Therefore according to Thy will
  Have mercy now on me.

O Jesu, oft it grieveth me.
  And troubleth sore my mind,
That I so weak and frail am found
  To wander with the blind.

O Jesu dear, Thou lasting light,
  Whose brightness doth excel;
The clearness of Thy beams send down
  Within my heart to dwell.

O Jesu, quicken Thou my soul
  That it may cleave to Thee;
And for Thy painful passion's sake
  Have mercy now on me.

THE CONCLUSION OF HIS "COMPLAINT OF OLD AGE."

Let us our course direct
  While perfect mind we have,
And set our compass towards Christ,
  Who only must us save.

Let Him from henceforth now
  Our only study be,
Our pleasant muse, our chief delight,
  Our joy and liberty.

Let us not care at all
  For worldly matters vain,
Nor for the body, so the soul
  With Jesus Christ remain.

While soul and body both
  Shall, at the Judgment Day,
United be and sentence hear
  Which Christ himself shall say;

Which grant, O Father dear,
  For Christ His sake, Thy Son,
May be unto our endless joy
  In life that is to come.

THOMAS TUSSER.

BORN ABOUT 1523; DIED ABOUT 1580.

THIS quaint writer was born at Rivenhall, near Witham in Essex. In his boyhood he was a chorister at St. Paul's, and completed his education at Eton and Trinity Hall, Cambridge. He afterwards became a retainer in the service of William, Lord Paget. Growing weary of a courtier's life, he retired into the country, and occupied himself with farming. Thomas Fuller says of him : " He was successively a musician, schoolmaster, serving man, husbandman, grazier, and poet: more skilful in all than thriving in any vocation. He traded at large in oxen, sheep, dairies, and grain of all kinds, to no profit. Whether he bought or sold, he lost; and as renter, impoverished himself and never enriched his landlord. Yet hath he laid down excellent rules in his book of husbandry and huswifery." His principal work is a poem, of which the first edition appeared in 1557, entitled, *A Hundred Points of Good Husbandry*. It went through many editions, and in 1573 was published in a greatly enlarged form, under the title of *Five Hundred Points of Good Husbanary united to as many of Good Huswifery*. It is said to be the earliest didactic poem in the English language. He died in London about 1580.

POSIES FOR THINE OWN BEDCHAMBER.

WHAT wisdom more, what better life, than pleaseth God to send?
What worldly goods, what longer use, than pleaseth God to lend?
What better fare than well-content, agreeing with thy wealth?
What better guest than trusty friend, in sickness and in health?
What better bed than conscience good, to pass the night with sleep?
What better work than daily care from sin thyself to keep?

What better thought than think on God, and daily Him to serve !
What better gift than to the poor, that ready be to sterve ?[1]
What greater praise of God and man than mercy for to show ?
Who, merciless, shall mercy find, that mercy shows to few ?
What worse despair than loath to die, for fear to go hell ?
What greater faith than trust in God, through Christ in heaven to
    dwell ?

OF THE OMNIPOTENCY OF GOD AND DEBILITY OF MAN.

O GOD, thou glorious God, what God is like to Thee !
What life, what strength, is like to Thine, as all the world may see ?
The heavens, the earth, the seas, and all Thy works therein,
Do show (to whom Thou would'st to know) that Thou hast ever been.

But all the thoughts of man are bent to wretched evil,
Man doth commit idolatry bewitched of the devil :
What ill is left undone where man may have his will—
Man ever was a hypocrite, and so continues still.

The joy that man hath here is as a spark of fire,
His acts be like the smould'ring smoke, himself like dirt and mire,
His strength ev'n as a reed, his age much like the flower,
His breath or life is but a puff, uncertain every hour.

But for the Holy Ghost, and for His gifts of grace,
The death of Christ, Thy mercy great, man were in woful case :
Oh grant us, therefore, Lord, to amend that is amiss,
And when from hence we do depart, to rest with Thee in bliss.

[1] Starve.

HUMPHREY GIFFORD.

NOTHING more seems known of this poet than his work entitled *A Posie of Gillyflowers*, published 1580.

THE LIFE OF MAN.
METAPHORICALLY COMPARED TO A SHIP SAILING ON THE SEAS IN A TEMPEST.

HASTE homewards, man; draw nearer to the shore;
   The skies do scowl, the winds do blow amain;
The ragged rocks with rumbling noise do roar,
   The foggy clouds do threaten storms of rain;
Each thing foreshows a tempest is at hand:
Hoist up thy sails and haste to happy land.

In worldly seas thy silly[1] ship is tost,
   With waves of woe beset on every side,
Blown here and there, in danger to be lost,
   Dark clouds of sin do cause thee wander wide;
Unless thy God on thee some pity take,
On rocks of ruth[2] thou needs must shipwreck make.

Cut down the mast of rancour and debate;
   Unfreight the ship of all unlawful wares;
Cast overboard the packs of hoarded hate,
   Pump out foul vice, the cause of many cares;
If that some leak it make thee stand in doubt,
Repentance serves to stop the water out.

      [1] Poor, weak.   [2] Sorrow.

"IN WORLDLY SEAS THY SILLY SHIP IS TOST,
WITH WAVES OF WOE BESET ON EVERY SIDE."

Let God's pure word thy line and compass be;
And steadfast faith weigh thou in anchor's stead:
Lament thy sins; then shalt thou shortly see
That power divine will help thee forth at need.
Fell Satan is chief ruler of these seas—
He seeks our wreck; he doth these tempests raise.

In what we may, let us alway repress
The furious waves of lust and strong desire;
A quiet calm our conscience shall possess,
If we do that which duty doth require:
By godly life, in fine, obtain we shall
The port of bliss: to which God send us all!

A PRAYER.

O MIGHTY God! which for us men didst suffer on the cross
The painful pangs of bitter death, to save our souls from loss,
I yield Thee here most hearty thanks, in that Thou dost vouchsafe
Of me, most vile and sinful wretch, so great regard to have.

Alas! none ever had more cause to magnify Thy name
Than I, to whom Thy mercies shown do witness well the same:
So many brunts of fretting foes who ever could withstand,
If Thou hadst not protected me with Thy most holy hand?

When as the Fiend had led my soul e'en to the gates of hell,
Thou call'dst me back and dost me choose in heaven with Thee
 to dwell.
Let Furies now fret on their fill, let Satan rage and roar,
As long as Thou art on my side what need I care for more?

"THE RAINBOW BENDING IN THE SKY."

GEORGE GASCOIGNE.

BORN A.D. ——— ; DIED A.D. 1577.

GASCOIGNE was the son of Sir John Gascoigne, of Walthamstow. In his early life he was guilty of many excesses, for which he is said to have been disinherited by his father. He studied at Cambridge, and was subsequently entered at Gray's Inn; but he soon abandoned the law and went abroad as a soldier. He received a commission from the Prince of Orange, but a quarrel with his superior officer caused him to return to England, and he entered the service of Queen Elizabeth. In his later years he displayed true and deep sorrow for his early follies, and retired to Walthamstow, where he died peacefully in 1577.

"GOOD MORROW."

You that have spent the silent night
    In sleep and quiet rest,
And love to see the cheerful light
    That riseth in the east,
Now clear your voice, now cheer your heart,
    Come help me now to sing;
Each willing wight come bear a part,
    To praise the heavenly King.

And you whom care in prison keeps,
    Or sickness doth suppress,
Or secret sorrow breaks your sleeps,
    Or dolours do distress,
Yet bear a part in doleful wise,
    Yea, think it good accord
And acceptable sacrifice,
    Each sprite to praise the Lord.

The dreadful night with darksomeness
    Hath overspread the light,
And sluggish sleep with drowsiness
    Hath overprest our might—
A glass wherein you may behold
    Each storm that stops our breath;
Our bed the grave, our clothes like mould,
    And sleep like dreadful death.

Yet as this deadly night did last
  But for a little space,
And heavenly day, now night is past,
  Doth show his pleasant face:
So must we hope to see God's face
  At last in heaven on high,
When we have changed this mortal place
  For immortality.

And of such haps and heavenly joys
  As then we hope to hold,
All earthly sights and worldly joys
  Are tokens to behold.
The day is like the day of doom,
  The sun, the Son of man,
The skies the heavens, the earth the tomb
  Wherein we rest till then.

The rainbow bending in the sky,
  Bedecked with sundry hues,
Is like the seat of God on high,
  And seems to tell this news:
That as thereby He promisèd
  To drown the world no more,
So, by the blood which Christ hath shed,
  He will our health restore.

The misty clouds that fall sometime
  And overcast the skies,
Are like to troubles of our time,
  Which do but dim our eyes:

But as such dews are dried up quite,
   When Phœbus shows his face,
So are such fancies put to flight
   When God doth guide by grace.

The little birds which sing so sweet
   Are like the angels' voice,
Which render God His praises meet
   And teach us to rejoice:
And as they more esteem that mirth
   Than dread the night's annoy,
So much we deem our days on earth
   But hell to heavenly joy.

Unto which joys for to attain,
   God grant us all His grace,
And send us, after worldly pain,
   In heaven to have a place,
Where we may still enjoy that light
   Which never shall decay:
Lord, for Thy mercy, lend us might
   To see that joyful day.

GOOD NIGHT.

WHEN thou hast spent the ling'ring day
   In pleasure and delight,
Or after toil and weary way
   Dost seek to rest at night,
Unto thy pains or pleasures past
   Add this one labour yet:
Ere sleep close up thine eye too fast,
   Do not thy God forget.

But search within thy secret thought
  What deeds did thee befall;
And if thou find amiss in aught,
  To God for mercy call.
Yea, though thou nothing find amiss
  Which thou canst call to mind,
Yet evermore remember this,
  There is the more behind.

And think, how well so e'er it be
  That thou hast spent the day,
It came of God, and not of thee,
  So to direct thy way.
Thus if thou try thy daily deeds,
  And pleasure in this pain,
Thy life shall cleanse thy corn from weeds,
  And thine shall be the gain.

SIR NICHOLAS BRETON.

DATE UNCERTAIN.

OF the history of Sir Nicholas Breton little is known beyond the fact that he formed one in that crowd of poets who made the era of Queen Elizabeth so illustrious in our literature. During his life, and for some time subsequently, his poems enjoyed great popularity, though they are now almost forgotten. His compositions are most of them religious in their character. From the melancholy tone which pervades them, he seems to have had a life of disappointment and sorrow.

FROM "THE SOUL'S HARMONY."

LORD, when I think how I offend Thy will,
   And know what good is in obedience to it,
And see my hurt, and yet continue still
   In doing ill, and cannot leave to do it;

And then again do feel that bitter smart,
   That inward breeds of pleasure's after-pain,
When scarce the thought is entered in my heart
   But it is gone and sin gets in again;

And when again the act of sin is past,
   And that Thy grace doth call me back again,
Then in my tears I run to Thee as fast,
   And of my sins and of myself complain;

      What can I do but cry, Sweet Jesus, save me!
      For I am nothing but what Thou wilt have me.

SIR NICHOLAS BRETON.

THE SOUL'S LONGINGS.

O GRACIOUS God, and Lord of mercy's might,
Why do I live amid this world of woe?
When every day doth seem to me as night,
While sorrows seek my spirit's overthrow.

I hear Thy word, and would obey Thy will,
But want the power that might perform my due;
I know the good, and fain would leave the ill,
And fear the sorrow that doth sin ensue.

And yet I fall into that depth of sin
That makes me fear the judgment of Thy wrath,
Until Thy grace doth all my help begin
To know what comfort faith in mercy hath.

O Blessed Light that shows in mercy's eye!
While faith doth live, that love can never die.

FAREWELL TO THE WORLD.

Go; bid the world, with all its trash, farewell!
And tell the earth it shall be all but dust.
These wicked wares that worldlings buy and sell,
The moth will eat or else the canker rust:
All flesh is grass, and to the grave it must.
This sink of sin is but the way to hell;
Leave it I say, and bid the world farewell.

Account of pomp but as a shadowed power,
  And think of friends but as the summer flies;
Esteem of beauty as a fading flower,
  And lovers' fancies but as fabled lies:
Know that on earth there is no paradise.
Who sees not heaven is surely spirit-blind,
And like a body that doth lack a mind.

Then let us lie as dead, till there we live,
  Where only love doth live for ever blest,
And only love the only life doth give
  That brings the soul into eternal rest:
Let us this wicked, wretched world detest,
Where graceless hearts in hellish sins persever,[1]
And fly to heaven, to live in grace for ever.

[1] Persevere.

SIR PHILIP SIDNEY ON THE FIELD OF ZUTPHEN.

SIR PHILIP SIDNEY.

BORN A.D. 1554; DIED A.D. 1586.

SIR PHILIP SIDNEY, the brightest ornament of the court of Elizabeth, was the son of Sir Henry Sidney of Penshurst, the favourite of King Edward VI., who expired in his arms. He was educated at Shrewsbury, and at Christ Church, Oxford. On leaving the University he went abroad and travelled extensively in various parts of Europe. He was in Paris on the night of the Massacre of St. Bartholomew, and took refuge in the house of Sir Francis Walsingham, the English Ambassador. He returned to England in 1575, and speedily gained the favour and confidence of Queen

Elizabeth (who called him "her Philip"), and the admiration and esteem of all classes, which he won not only by the beauty of his person, the charm of his manners, and the brilliancy of his accomplishments, but by the purity and integrity of his life. So great was his reputation abroad, as well as at home, that the crown of Poland is said to have been offered him. He served in the Netherlands under the Earl of Leicester, where he was appointed Governor of Flushing, and General of the Horse. He died of a wound received in a skirmish at Zutphen, at the early age of thirty-two. It was after receiving his mortal wound that the well-known incident occurred, thus narrated by his friend, Lord Brooke. "Being thirsty with excess of bleeding, he called for some drink, which was presently brought him; but as he was putting the bottle to his mouth he saw a poor soldier carried along, who had eaten his last at the same feast, ghastly casting up his eyes at the same bottle. Which Sir Philip perceiving took it from his head before he drank, and delivered it to the poor man with these words: 'Thy necessity is yet greater than mine!'" The intelligence of his death caused universal lamentation throughout Europe, and he received the honour of a public funeral. Assisted by his accomplished sister the Countess of Pembroke, he wrote a metrical version of the Psalms, one or two specimens of which are given, more on account of their authorship than for their intrinsic merit.

PS. CXXXIII.

How good, and how beseeming well
   It is that we,
   Who brethren be,
As brethren should in concord dwell!

Like that dear oil that Aaron bears
   Which, fleeting down
   To foot from crown,
Embalms his head and robe he wears.

Or like the tears the morn doth shed,
   Which lie on ground
   Empearled round,
On Sion or on Hermon's head.

For joined therewith the Lord doth give
Such grace, such bliss,
That where it is
Men may for ever blessed live.

PS. CXXXIX.

O LORD, in me there lieth nought
But to Thy search revealed lies;
For when I sit
Thou markest it,
No less Thou notest when I rise;
Yea, closest closet of my thought
Hath open windows to Thine eyes.

Thou walkest with me when I walk,
When to my bed for rest I go,
I find Thee there
And everywhere;
Not youngest thought in me doth grow,
No, not one word I cast to talk,
But yet unuttered Thou dost know.

To shun Thy notice, leave Thine eye,
Oh, whither might I take my way?
To starry sphere?
Thy throne is there:
To dead men's undelightsome stay?
There is thy walk, and there to lie
Unknown in vain I should essay.

O Sun! whom light nor flight can match,
Suppose thy lightful, flightful wings
   Thou lend to me,
   And I could flee
As far as thee the evening brings;
E'en led to west He would me catch,
Nor should I lurk with western things.

Do thou thy best, O secret night!
In sable veil to cover me :
   The sable veil
   Shall vainly fail,
With day unmasked my night shall be :
For night is day, and darkness light,
O Father of all lights, to Thee.

PS. XCVI.

Sing, and let the song be new,
   Unto Him that never endeth :
Sing all earth, and all in you :
Sing to God and bless His name,
   Of the help, the health He sendeth,
Day by day new ditties frame.

Make each country know His worth :
   Of His acts the wondrous story
Paint unto each people forth :
For Jehovah great alone,
   All the gods, for awe and glory,
Far above doth hold His throne.

Go, adore Him in the place
  Where His pomp is most displayed;
Earth, oh go with quaking pace,
Go, proclaim Jehovah King:
  Stayless world shall now be stayed;
Righteous doom His rule shall bring.

Starry roof and earthy floor,
  Sea, and all thy wideness yieldeth,
Now rejoice, and leap, and roar.
Leafy infants of the wood,
  Fields and all that on you feedeth,
Dance, oh dance at such a good.

For Jehovah cometh, lo!
  Lo! to reign Jehovah cometh;
Under whom you all shall go:
He the world shall rightly guide;
  Truly, as a King becometh,
For the people's weal provide.

SPENSER.

EDMUND SPENSER.

BORN A.D. 1553; DIED A.D. 1599.

THIS illustrious poet was a native of London, and received his University education at Cambridge, where he was admitted as a sizar of Pembroke Hall. In 1578 he returned to London, and was introduced to Sir Philip Sidney, whose intimate friend he at once became; residing with him at Penshurst, and acting as his secretary. On Sidney's untimely death, Spenser helped by his verse to express the general sorrow. He says,—

>He, only like himself,
>Was second unto none,
>Whose death (though life) we rue and wrong,
>And all in vain do moan

> Their loss—not him—wail they
> That fill the world with cries;
> Death slew not him, but he made death
> His ladder to the skies.

In 1580 Spenser accompanied Lord Grey of Wilton, Lord-Lieutenant of Ireland, to that country, as his secretary. He returned with him to England in 1583, and again went out to Ireland in 1586, having received a grant of land on the condition of his residing on it; which he did in Kilcolman Castle, in the county of Cork. It must have been an uncongenial abode; to go there then was like going into banishment. The country was an uncultivated waste, and the people were little better than savages'; yet there the greater part of the Fairy Queen was composed, which he describes as,

> Rude rhymes, the which a rustic muse did weave
> In savage soil far from Parnasso Mount.

He speaks of a visit which he received here from Sir Walter Raleigh, in a way which shows how delightful it must have been to him, in his retirement, to welcome such a guest. Raleigh persuaded him to return with him to London, and introduced him at Court. He received as the result of this visit, a pension of £50 a year. On his return to Ireland in 1594, he married. In 1596 he again came to England, bringing three fresh books of the Fairy Queen. We have a proof that he was not an inattentive observer of what was going on around him, in his able and interesting work "On the State of Ireland," written about this time. In 1597 he again went to Ireland, but not for long. In the following year Tyrone's rebellion began to rage. The ferocious rebels attacked and burned his house; he and his wife escaped, but their infant child perished in the flames. He returned to London a broken-hearted man; and died in great poverty at Westminster, January 16, 1599. He was buried in the Abbey, at the charge of the Earl of Essex, who caused this inscription to be placed on his tomb.

"Here lies (expecting the second coming of our Saviour Christ Jesus) the body of Edmund Spenser, the prince of poets in his time, whose divine spirit needs no other witness than the works he left behind him."

Great indeed is the witness which they bear to the poetic genius and ever fertile imagination which have made them an inexhaustible spring of thought and diction for the greatest of his successors. More in accordance with our present object is it to notice that they bear witness also to the reverential Christian spirit in which he exercised his wonderful gifts. Few of his poems of a directly religious character are extant. Some extracts from two which remain—the Hymns to Heavenly Love and Beauty—are given here. The Fairy Queen contains many deep religious truths couched in the form of allegory, and the careful reader of the First Book will be

THE RED CROSS KNIGHT AT THE HOUSE OF HOLINESS.

interested to find how it contains the germ of the thoughts afterwards carried out and perfected by John Bunyan in the Pilgrim's Progress. Amongst these may be noticed the description of Despair, and his advice to the Red-cross Knight to commit suicide; the House of Holiness, where the Knight is admitted by the porter Humility, tended by the three maidens, Faith, Hope, and Charity, and comforted by "an ancient matron named Mercy." He there receives various lessons from them, and from the top of a hill an old man points out to him a distant view of the heavenly city. A few stanzas from this canto are given below.

THE RED-CROSS KNIGHT AT THE HOUSE OF HOLINESS.

Arrived there, the door they find fast locked;
For it was warely watchèd, night and day,
For fear of many foes; but when they knocked,
The porter opened unto them straightway.
He was an aged sire all hoary gray,
With looks full lowly cast, and gait full slow,
Wont on a staff his feeble steps to stay,
Hight Humilta. They pass in, stooping low;
For strait and narrow was the way which he did show.
  *   *   *   *   *   *
Now when their weary limbs with kindly rest,
And bodies were refreshed with due repast,
Fair Una 'gan Fidelia fair request
To have her knight within her school-house placed,
That of her heavenly learning he might taste,
And hear the wisdom of her words divine.
She granted; and that knight so much a-graced
That she him taught celestial discipline,
And opened his dull eyes that light might in them shine;

And that her sacred book, with blood y-writt,
That none could read except she them did teach,
She unto him disclosèd every whit,
And heavenly documents thereout did preach,
That weaker wit of man could never reach,
Of God, of grace, of justice, of freewill:
That wonder was to hear her godly speech;
For she was able with her words to kill,
And raise again to life the heart that she did thrill.

And when she list pour out her larger sprite,[1]
She would command the hasty sun to stay,
Or backward turn his course from heaven's height:
Sometimes great hosts of men she could dismay;
Dryshod to pass she parts the floods in tway;
And eke huge mountains from their native seat
She would command themselves to bear away,
And throw in raging sea with roaring threat:
Almighty God her gave such power and puissance great.

The faithful knight now grew, in little space,
By hearing her, and by her sister's lore,
To such perfection of all heavenly grace,
That wretched world he 'gan for to abhore,
And mortal life 'gan loath as thing forlore;
Grieved with remembrance of his wicked ways,
And pricked with anguish of his sins so sore,
That he desired to end his wretched days:
So much the dart of sinful guilt the soul dismays!

But wise Speranza gave him comfort sweet,
And taught him how to take assurèd hold

[1] Spirit.

Upon her silver anchor, as was meet;
Else had his sins, so great and manifold,
Made him forget all that Fidelia told.
* * * * *
From thence, far off he unto him did show
A little path, that was both steep and long,
Which to a goodly city led his view;
Whose walls and towers were builded high and strong
Of pearl and precious stone, that earthly tongue
Cannot describe, nor wit of man can tell;
Too high a ditty for my simple song!
The city of the Great King hight it well,
Wherein eternal peace and happiness doth dwell.

As he thereon stood gazing, he might see
The blessed angels to and fro descend
From highest heaven in gladsome company,
And with great joy into that city wend,
As commonly as friend does with his friend.
Whereat he wondered much, and 'gan inquire,
What stately building durst so high extend
Her lofty towers unto the starry sphere,
And what unknowen nation there empeopled were.

Fair knight, quoth he, Jerusalem that is,
The New Jerusalem that God hath built
For those to dwell in that are chosen His,
His chosen people purged from sinful guilt
With precious blood, which cruelly was spilt
On cursed tree, of that unspotted Lamb
That for the sins of all the world was killed:
Now are they saints all in that city sam,[1]
More dear unto their God than younglings to their dam.

[1] Together.

THE MINISTRY OF ANGELS.

AND is there care in heaven? and is there love
In heavenly spirits to these creatures base,
That may compassion of their evils move?
There is—else much more wretched were the case
Of men than beasts: but oh the exceeding grace
Of highest God, that loves His creatures so,
And all His works with mercy doth embrace,
That blessed angels He sends to and fro,
To serve to wicked man, to serve His wicked foe!

How oft do they their silver bowers leave
To come to succour us that succour want!
How oft do they with golden pinions cleave
The flitting skies, like flying pursuivant,
Against foul fiends to aid us militant!
They for us fight, they watch and duly ward,
And their bright squadrons round about us plant;
And all for love, and nothing for reward:
Oh why should heavenly God to men have such regard?

HYMN ON HEAVENLY LOVE.

LOVE, lift me up upon thy golden wings
From this base world unto thy heaven's height,
Where I may see those admirable things
Which there thou workest by thy sovereign might,

Far above feeble reach of earthly sight,
That I thereof a heavenly hymn may sing
Unto the God of love, high heaven's King.

*   *   *   *   *

O blessed Well of Love! O Flower of Grace!
O glorious Morning Star! O Lamp of Light!
Most lively image of Thy Father's face,
Eternal King of Glory, Lord of Might,
Meek Lamb of God before all worlds behight,[1]
How can we Thee requite for all this good?
Or what can prize that Thy most precious blood?

Yet nought Thou ask'st in lieu of all this love,
But love of us, for guerdon of Thy pain.
Ay me! what can us less than that behove?
Had He requirèd life of us again,
Had it been wrong to ask His own again?
He gave us life, He it restored us lost;
Then life were least that us so little cost.

But He our life hath left unto us free,
Free that was thrall, and blessèd that was banned;[2]
Nor ought demands but that we loving be,
As He himself hath loved us aforehand,
And bound thereto with an eternal band,
Him first to love that us so dearly bought,s
And next our brethren to His image wrought.

*   *   *   *

Then rouse thyself, O earth, out of thy soil,
In which thou wallowest like to filthy swine,
And dost thy mind in dirty pleasures moil,

---

[1] Named.   [2] Cursed.

Unmindful of that dearest Lord of thine!
Lift up to Him thy heavy, clouded eyne,
That thou this sovereign bounty may'st behold,
And read through love His mercies manifold.

Begin from first where He encradled was
In simple cratch, wrapt in a wad of hay,
Between the wilful ox and humble ass,
And in what rags, and in how base array,
The glory of our heavenly riches lay,
When Him the silly[1] shepherds came to see,
Whom greatest princes sought on lowest knee.

From thence read on the story of His life,
His humble carriage, His unfaulty ways,
His cankered foes, His fights, His toil, His strife,
His pains, His poverty, His sharp assays,
Through which He passed His miserable days,
Offending none, and doing good to all,
Yet being maliced both of great and small.

And look, at last, how of most wretched wights
He taken was, betrayed, and false accused,
How with most scornful taunts, and fell despites
He was reviled, disgraced, and foul abused;
How scourged, how crowned, how buffeted, how bruised;
And, lastly, how 'twixt robbers crucified,
With bitter wounds, through hands, through feet, and side.

Then let thy flinty heart, that feels no pain,
Empiercèd be with pitiful remorse,
And let thy bowels bleed in every vein,

[1] Simple.

At sight of His most sacred heavenly corse,
So torn and mangled with malicious force;
And let thy soul, whose sins His sorrows wrought,
Melt into tears, and groan in grievèd thought.

THE WISE MEN ENTERING BETHLEHEM.

With sense whereof, while thy so softened spirit
Is inly touched and humbled with meek zeal,
Through meditation of His endless merit,
Lift up thy mind to th' Author of thy weal.

And to His sovereign mercy do appeal;
Learn Him to love that lovèd thee so dear,
And in thy breast His blessèd image bear.

With all thy heart, with all thy soul and mind,
Thou must Him love, and His behests embrace;
All other loves, with which the world doth blind
Weak fancies, and stir up affections base,
Thou must renounce and utterly displace,
And give thyself unto Him full and free,
That fully, freely gave Himself to thee.

Then shalt thou feel thy spirit so possessed,
And ravished with devouring great desire
Of His dear self, that shall thy feeble breast
Inflame with love, and set thee all on fire
With burning zeal, through every part entire,
That in no earthly thing thou shalt delight,
But in His sweet and amiable sight.

Thenceforth all world's desire will in thee die,
And all earth's glory, on which men do gaze,
Seem dust and dross in thy pure-sighted eye,
Compared to that celestial beauty's blaze,
Whose glorious beams all fleshly sense doth daze
With admiration of their passing light,
Blinding the eyes, and 'lumining the sprite.

Then shall thy ravished soul inspired be
With heavenly thoughts, far above human skill,
And thy bright radiant eyes shall plainly see
Th' idea of His pure glory present still

Before thy face, that all thy spirit shall fill
With sweet enragement of celestial love,
Kindled through sight of those fair things above.

HEAVENLY BEAUTY.

CEASE then, my tongue, and lend unto my mind
Leave to bethink how great that beauty is,
Whose utmost parts so beautiful I find:
How much more those essential parts of His,
His truth, His love, His wisdom, and His bliss,
His grace, His doom, His mercy, and His might,
By which He lends us of Himself a sight.

Those unto all He daily doth display,
And show Himself in th' image of His grace,
As in a looking-glass, through which He may
Be seen of all His creatures vile and base,
That are unable else to see His face;
His glorious face! which glistereth else so bright,
That th' angels selves cannot endure His sight.

But we, frail wights! whose sight cannot sustain
The sun's bright beams, when he on us doth shine,
But that their points rebutted back again
Are dulled, how can we see with feeble eyne
The glory of that Majesty Divine,
In sight of whom both sun and moon are dark,
Comparèd to His least resplendent spark!

Humbled with fear and awful reverence,
Before the footstool of His majesty
Throw thyself down with trembling innocence,
Nor dare look up with corruptible eye
On the dread face of that great Deity,
For fear, lest if He chance to look on thee,
Thou turn to nought, and quite confounded be.

But lowly fall before His mercy-seat,
Close covered with the Lamb's integrity
From the just wrath of His avengeful threat
That sits upon the righteous throne on high:
His throne is built upon eternity;
More firm and durable than steel or brass,
Or the hard diamond, which them both doth pass.

His sceptre is the rod of righteousness,
With which He bruiseth all His foes to dust,
And the great dragon strongly doth repress,
Under the rigour of his judgment just;
His seat is truth, to which the faithful trust,
From whence proceed her beams so pure and bright,
That all about Him sheddeth glorious light.

* * * *

Ah, then, my hungry soul! which long hast fed
On idle fancies of thy foolish thought,
And, with false beauty's flattering bait misled,
Hast after vain deceitful shadows sought,
Which all are fled, and now have left thee nought
But late repentance through thy folly's prief;[1]
Ah! cease to gaze on matter of thy grief:

[1] Proof.

And look at last up to that sovereign light,
From whose pure beams all perfect beauty springs,
That kindleth love in every godly sprite,
Even the love of God; which loathing brings
Of this vile world and these gay-seeming things;
With whose sweet pleasures being so possest,
Thy straying thoughts henceforth for ever rest.

FROM "THE WORLD'S VANITY."

LOOKING far forth into the ocean wide,
A goodly ship, with banners bravely dight,[1]
And flag in her top-gallant, I espied,
Through the main sea making her merry flight:
Fair blew the wind into her bosom right;
And the heavens looked lovely all the while;
That she did seem to dance as in delight,
And at her own felicity did smile.
All suddenly there clove unto her keel
A little fish, that men call Remora,
Which stopped her course, and held her by the heel,
That wind nor tide could move her thence away.
Strange thing, me seemeth, that so small a thing
Should able be so great a one to wring.

A mighty lion, lord of all the wood,
Having his hunger thoroughly satisfied
With prey of beasts and spoil of living blood,
Safe in his dreadless den him sought to hide:
His sternness was his praise, his strength his pride,

---

[1] Decked.

"A MIGHTY LION, LORD OF ALL THE WOOD."

And all his glory in his cruel claws.
I saw a wasp, that fiercely him defied,
And bade him battle, even to his jaws :
Sore he him stung, that it the blood forth draws,
And his proud heart is filled with fretting ire :
In vain he threats his teeth, his tail, his paws,
And from his bloody eyes doth sparkle fire ;
That dead himself he wisheth for despite ;
So weakest may annoy the most of might !

When these sad sights were overpast and gone,
My sprite was greatly movèd in her rest,
With inward ruth and dear affection,
To see so great things by so small distrest :
Thenceforth I 'gan in my engrieved breast
To scorn all difference of great and small,
Sith that the greatest often are opprest,
And unawares do into danger fall.
And ye, that read these ruins tragical,
Learn, by their loss, to love the low degree ;
And, if that fortune chance you up to call
To Honour's seat, forget not what you be :
For he, that of himself is most secure,
Shall find his state most fickle and unsure.

GILES FLETCHER.

BORN 1588; DIED 1623.

GILES FLETCHER was the eldest son of Dr. Giles Fletcher, who was ambassador to Russia in the reign of Elizabeth, and who enjoyed some reputation as a poet and scholar in his own day, though now forgotten. The son was educated at Trinity College, Cambridge; and being appointed to the living of Alderton, in Suffolk, he lived there till his death in 1623. His chief poem was an allegory, entitled *Christ's Victory and Triumph, in Heaven and Earth, over and after Death*. Though not quite free from tedium and obscurity in some of the passages, it yet deserves to be better known than it is. Southey esteemed it very highly, and said that it would "preserve the author's name whilst there was any praise."

"AFTER THEY HAD SUNG A HYMN, THEY WENT OUT UNTO THE MOUNT OF OLIVES."

AND yet how can I hear Thee singing go,
When men, incensed with hate, Thy death foreset?
Or else, why do I hear Thee sighing so,
When Thou, inflamed with love, their life dost get;
That love and hate, and sighs and songs are met?
  But thus, and only thus, Thy love did crave,
  To send Thee singing for us to the grave,
When we sought Thee to kill, and Thou sought'st us to save.

When I remember Christ our burden bears,
I look for glory, and find misery;
I look for joy, and find a sea of tears;
I look that we should live, and find Him die;

I look for angels' songs, and hear Him cry:
Thus what I look, I cannot find so well;
Or rather, what I find I cannot tell,
These banks so narrow are, these streams so highly swell.

Christ suffers, and in this His tears begin,
Suffers for us, and our joy springs in this;
Suffers to death, here is His manhood seen;
Suffers to rise, and here His Godhead is;
For man that could not by himself have risen,
   Out of the grave doth by the Godhead rise,
   And God, that could not die, in manhood dies,
That we in both might live by that sweet sacrifice.

Go, giddy brains, whose wits are thought so fresh,
Pluck all the flowers that Nature forth doth throw;
Go stick them on the cheek of wanton flesh:
Poor idol, forced at once to fall and grow!
Of fading roses and of melting snow
   Your songs exceed your matter; this of mine
   The matter which it sings shall make divine,
As stars dull puddles gild in which they shine.
                From "Christ's Triumph over Death"

CHRIST'S ASCENSION.

"Toss up your heads, ye everlasting gates,
And let the Prince of Glory enter in;
At whose great volley of sidereal states,
The sun to blush and stars grow pale were seen;

When leaping first from earth, He did begin
To climb His angel's wings. Then open hang
Your crystal doors!"—So all the chorus sang
Of heavenly birds, as to the stars they nimbly sprang.

Hark how the floods clap their applauding hands,
The pleasant valleys singing for delight,
And wanton mountains dance about the lands,
The while the fields, struck with the heavenly light,
Set all their flowers a-smiling at the sight;
　　The trees laugh with their blossoms, and the sound
　　Of the triumphant shout of praise, that crowned
The flaming Lamb, breaking through heaven hath passage found.

Out leap the antique patriarchs all in haste,
To see the powers of hell in triumph led,
And with small stars a garland interchased
Of olive leaves they bore to crown His head,
That was before with thorns deglorièd:
　　After them flew the prophets, brightly stoled
　　In shining lawn, and wimpled manifold,
Striking their ivory harps, strung all in cords of gold.

To which the saints victorious carols sung,
Ten thousand saints at once, that with the sound
The hollow vaults of heaven for triumph rung:
The cherubim their clamours did confound
With all the rest, and clapped their wings around:
　　Down from their thrones the dominations flew,
　　And at His feet their crowns and sceptres throw,
And all the princely souls fell on their faces low.

Nor can the martyrs' wounds them stay behind,
But out they rush among the heavenly crowd,
Seeking their heaven out of their heaven to find,
Sounding their silver trumpets out so loud,
That the shrill noise broke through the starry cloud,
    And all the virgin souls, in pure array,
    Came dancing forth and making joyous play;
So Him they led along into the courts of day.

So Him they led into the courts of day,
Where never war nor wounds abide Him more,
But in that house eternal peace doth play,
Acquieting the souls, that, new before,
Their way to heaven through their own blood did score,
    But now, estrangèd from all misery
    As far as heaven and earth diswasted lie,
Swelter in quiet waves of immortality.

                From "Christ's Triumph after Death."

PHINEAS FLETCHER.

BORN ABOUT A.D. 1584; DIED ABOUT A.D. 1650.

PHINEAS, younger brother of Giles Fletcher, and like him a country clergyman. He was rector of Hilgay in Norfolk for twenty-nine years. His principal poem was an allegory in twelve books, entitled *The Purple Island*. The following extract will suffice to show how closely he copied Spenser.

ALLEGORICAL DESCRIPTION OF HUMILITY AND FAITH.

NEXT Tapinus,[1] whose sweet, though lowly grace,
All other higher than himself esteemed;
He in himself prized things as mean and base,
Which yet in others great and glorious seemed;
   All ill due debt, good undeserved he thought,
   His heart a low-roofed house, but sweetly wrought,
Where God Himself would dwell, though He it dearly bought.

Honour he shuns, yet is the way unto him;
As hell he hates advancement won with bribes,
But public place and charge are forced to woo him;
But good to grace, ill to desert ascribes;
   Him (as his Lord) contents a lowly room,
   Whose first house was the blessèd Virgin's womb,
The next a cratch, the third a cross, the fourth a tomb.

So choicest drugs in meanest shrubs are found;
So precious gold in deepest centre dwells;
So sweetest violets trail on lowly ground;
So richest pearls lie closed in violet shells:

[1] Humility.

So lowest dales we let at highest rates;
So creeping strawberries yield daintiest cates,
The Highest highly loves the low, the lofty hates.

Upon his shield was drawn that shepherd lad
Who with a sling threw down faint Israel's fears;
And in his hand, his spoils and trophies glad,
The monster's sword and head, he bravely bears;

"SO LOWEST DALES WE LET AT HIGHEST RATES."

Plain in his lovely face you might behold
A blushing meekness met with courage bold:
Little, not little worth, was fairly wrought in gold.
  * * * *
By them went Fidé[1] marshall of the field;
Weak was his mother when she gave him day;

[1] Faith.

And he, at first, a sick and weakly child
As e'er with tears welcomed the sunny ray;
   Yet when more years afford more growth and might,
   A champion stout he was, and puissant knight,
As ever came in field or shone in armour bright.

So we may see a little lionet,
When newly whelped, a weak and tender thing,
Despised by every beast; but waxen great,
When fuller times full strength and courage bring,
   The beasts all crouching low, their king adore,
   And dare not see what they contemned before;
The humbling forest quakes at his affrighted roar.

Mountains he flings in seas with mighty hand;[1]
Stops and turns back the sun's impetuous course;
Nature breaks Nature's laws at his command;
No force of hell or heaven withstands his force;
   Events to come yet many ages hence,
   He present makes, by wondrous prescience;
Proving the senses blind, by being blind to sense.

His sky-like arms, dyed all in blue and white,
And set with golden stars that flaméd wide.
His shield invisible to mortal sight,
Yet he upon it easily descried
   The lively semblance of his dying Lord,
   Whose bleeding side with wicked steel was gored;
Which to his fainting spirits new courage would afford.

Strange was the force of that enchanted shield,
Which highest powers to it from heaven impart:

---

[1] Compare Spenser's description, page 34.

For who could bear it well, and rightly wield,
It saved from sword and spear and poisoned dart:
Well might he slip, and yet not wholly fall:
No final loss his courage might appall;
Growing more sound by wounds, and rising by his fall.

VERSION OF PSALM CXXX.

From the deeps of grief and fear,
O Lord! to Thee my soul repairs:
From Thy heaven bow down Thine ear;
Let Thy mercy meet my prayers.
    Oh if Thou mark'st
    What's done amiss,
    What soul so pure,
    Can see Thy bliss?

But with Thee sweet mercy stands,
Sealing pardons, working fear:
Wait, my soul, wait on His hands;
Wait mine eye, Oh! wait mine ear:
    If He His eye
    Or tongue affords,
    Watch all His looks,
    Catch all His words.

As a watchman waits for day,
And looks for light, and looks again;
When the night grows cold and gray,
To be relieved he calls amain:

So look, so wait,
So long mine eyes,
To see my Lord
My Sun, arise.

Wait, ye saints, wait on our Lord:
For from His tongue sweet mercy flows:
Wait on His cross, wait on His word;
Upon that tree redemption grows:
   He will redeem
   His Israel
   From sin and wrath,
   From death and hell.

GEOFFREY WHITNEY.

ABOUT A.D. 1586.

WHITNEY is only known as the author of a work called "*A Choice of Emblems for the most part gathered out of sundry Writers; Englished and moralized, and divers newly devized.*" From one of the Emblems being inscribed "To my countrymen of the Namptwiche in Cheshire," he seems to have been a native of that place. Each of the Emblems is illustrated by a woodcut, of which the poetry is descriptive and explanatory.

EMBLEM X.

A WOOD-CUTTER AT WORK.

Motto.—Soli Deo Gloria.[1]

HERE man with axe doth cut the bough in twain,
And without him the axe could nothing do;
Within the tool there doth no force remain,
But man it is that might doth put thereto:
  Like to this axe is man in all his deeds,
  Who hath no strength but what from God proceeds.

Then let him not make vaunt of his desert,
Nor brag thereof when he good deeds hath done,
For it is God that worketh in his heart,
And, with His grace, to good doth make him run.
  And of himself he weak thereto doth live,
  And God gives power, to whom all glory give.

[1] Glory to God alone.

EMBLEM XII.

A MOWER.

Motto,—Superest quod supra est.[1]

Adieu, deceitful world, thy pleasures I detest;
Now others with thy shows delude, my hope in heaven doth rest.

E'EN as a flower, or like unto the grass
Which now doth stand, and straight with scythe doth fall;
So is our state: now here, now hence we pass;
For time attends with shredding[2] scythe for all,
  And Death at length both old and young doth strike,
  And into dust doth turn us all alike.

Yet if we mark how swift our race doth run,
And weigh the cause why we created be;
Then shall we know, when that this life is done,
We shall be sure our country right to see.
  For here we are but strangers that must flit:
  The nearer home, the nearer to the pit.

Oh happy they that pondering this aright,
Before that here their pilgrimage be past,
Resign this world, and march with all their might
Within that path that leads where joys shall last;
  And while they may, there treasure up their store,
  Where without rust it lasts for evermore.

This world must change; that world shall still endure:
Here pleasures fade; there they shall endless be:
Here man doth sin; and there he shall be pure:
Here death he tastes; and there shall never die:
  Here hath he grief, and there shall joys possess
  As none hath seen, nor any heart can guess.

[1] What is above survives.   [2] Paring off.

SIR WALTER RALEIGH.

BORN A.D. 1552; BEHEADED A.D. 1618.

THE life of this distinguished man was marked by the extremes of prosperity and adversity, and by a romantic variety of incident only possible in an age when the same person could be soldier, sailor, politician, geographical discoverer, mining adventurer, historian, and poet. Born of an old Devonshire family and educated at Oxford, he stood high in the favour of Queen Elizabeth, in whose reign he served with distinction as a soldier in France and the Netherlands. As a navigator, he discovered and took possession of a large tract of country in America, which he named Virginia in honour of the virgin Queen. He represented Devonshire in Parliament, and had a share in the repulse of the Spanish Armada. On the accession of James the First he was tried and condemned on a charge of high treason, and was a prisoner in the Tower for twelve years, where he composed his great work, "The History of the World." He was released conditionally, that he might make an expedition to Guiana, where he hoped to establish mining operations: his expectations were disappointed, and returning unsuccessful he was executed under the sentence passed fifteen years before. The poetry of this remarkable man bears all the marks of his genius. The well-known piece, commonly ascribed to Raleigh, which stands first is, the outpouring of a soul which had learned, by bitter experience, the hollowness of earthly things, and was tempted to look only on the dark side. We feel that something is wanting, and the short pieces which follow show that Raleigh knew where to find that peace which the world cannot give.

THE FAREWELL.

Go, soul, the body's guest,
Upon a thankless errand ;
Fear not to touch the best ;
The truth shall be thy warrant.
Go, since I needs must die,
And give them all the lie.

Go, tell the court it glows
   And shines like painted wood;
Go, tell the church it shows
   What's good, but does no good.
      If court and church reply,
      Give court and church the lie.

Tell potentates they live
   Acting; but oh their actions!
Not loved, unless they give;
   Nor strong, but by their factions.
      If potentates reply,
      Give potentates the lie.

Tell men of high condition,
   That rule affairs of state,
Their purpose is ambition;
   Their practice only hate.
      And if they do reply,
      Then give them all the lie.

Tell those that brave it most,
   They beg for more by spending;
Who in their greatest cost
   Seek nothing but commending.
      And if they make reply,
      Spare not to give the lie.

Tell zeal it lacks devotion;
   Tell love it is but lust;
Tell time it is but motion;
   Tell flesh it is but dust:
      And wish them not reply,
      For thou must give the lie.

Tell age it daily wasteth;
  Tell honour how it alters;
Tell beauty that it blasteth;
  Tell favour that she falters:
    And as they do reply,
    Give every one the lie.

Tell wit how much it wrangles
  In tickle points of niceness;
Tell wisdom she entangles
  Herself in over-wiseness:
    And if they do reply,
    Then give them both the lie.

Tell physic of her boldness;
  Tell skill it is pretension;
Tell charity of coldness;
  Tell law it is contention:
    And if they yield reply,
    Then give them still the lie.

Tell fortune of her blindness;
  Tell nature of decay;
Tell friendship of unkindness;
  Tell justice of delay:
    And if they do reply,
    Then give them all the lie.

So when thou hast, as I
  Commanded thee, done blabbing,
Although to give the lie
  Deserves no less than stabbing;
    Yet stab at thee who will,
    No stab the soul can kill!

"HYMN."

Rise, O my soul, with thy desires to heaven,
And with divinest contemplation use
Thy time where time's eternity is given,
And let vain thoughts no more thy thoughts abuse;
   But down in darkness let them lie:
   So live thy better, let thy worse thoughts die!

And thou, my soul, inspir'd with holy flame,
View and review, with most regardful eye,
That holy cross, whence thy salvation came,
On which thy Saviour and thy sin did die!
   For in that sacred object is much pleasure,
   And in that Saviour is my life, my treasure.

To Thee, O Jesu! I direct my eye,
To Thee my hands, to Thee my humble knees;
To Thee my heart shall offer sacrifice,
To Thee my thoughts, who my thoughts only sees:
   To Thee myself, myself and all, I give;
   To Thee I die, to Thee I only live.

LINES WRITTEN THE NIGHT BEFORE HIS EXECUTION.

E'en such is time, that takes on trust
Our youth, our joys, our all we have,
And pays us but with age and dust;
Who in the dark and silent grave,

SIR WALTER RALEIGH IN THE TOWER.

When we have wandered all our ways,
Shuts up the story of our days.
But from this earth, this grave, this dust,
The Lord shall raise me up, I trust.

HIS PILGRIMAGE.

GIVE me my scallop—shell of quiet
My staff of faith to rest upon;
My scrip of joy, immortal diet;
My bottle of salvation;
My gown of glory (hope's true gage),
And thus I'll take my pilgrimage.

Blood must be my body's balmer,
No other balm will here be given,
Whilst my soul, like quiet palmer,
Travels to the land of heaven,
Over all the silver mountains,
Where do spring those nectar fountains :

And I there will sweetly kiss
The happy bowl of peaceful bliss,
Drinking mine eternal fill,
Flowing on each milky hill.
My soul will be athirst before,
But after, it will thirst no more.

JAMES SHIRLEY.

BORN A.D. 1596; DIED A.D. 1666.

THE three following stanzas, which give such a spirited and forcible description of the vanity of earthly things, are from the pen of James Shirley, a dramatist of note in the reign of Charles I. He was of Cambridge University, and a clergyman at St. Albans, but resigned his living, and followed literary pursuits. His house was burnt in the great fire of London, and in the following month he and his wife both died, it is said, from the effects of the fright and fatigue which they then experienced. In a collection of old ballads in the British Museum, there is one of ten stanzas, the first three of which are Shirley's; the other seven seem to have been added to point out the remedy for the evil described by him. But though the intention is good, the verses are quite destitute of the poetical vigour of the first three, and are not worth printing here.

THE VANITY OF VAIN GLORY.

THE glories of our birth and state
    Are shadows, not substantial things;
There is no armour against fate;
    Death lays his icy hand on kings.
Sceptre and crown must tumble down,
And in the dust be equal laid
With the poor crooked scythe and spade.

Some men with swords do reap the field,
    And plant fresh laurels where they kill;
But their strong nerves at length must yield—
    They tame but one another still.
Early or late they bend to fate,
    And must yield up their murmuring breath,
Whilst the pale captive bleeds to death.

The garland withers on your brow,
　Then boast no more your mighty deeds,
For on death's purple altar now
　See how the victor victim bleeds.
All heads must come to the cold tomb ;
Only the actions of the just
Smell sweet and blossom in the dust.

SIR JOHN DAVIES.

BORN A.D. 1570; DIED A.D. 1626.

SIR JOHN DAVIES, the son of a lawyer at Tisbury, in Wiltshire, was educated at Queen's College, Oxford. He became a member of the Middle Temple, and rose to eminence as a lawyer and politician. He sat in Parliament as member for Newcastle-under-Lyme, was for some time a judge in Ireland, and was in expectation of being made Chief Justice of England, when he died suddenly, at the age of fifty-six, A.D. 1626. His principal poem is called "*Nosce Teipsum: of the Soul of Man, and the Immortality thereof*." It was published in 1592, and dedicated to Queen Elizabeth.

MAN'S IGNORANCE OF HIMSELF.

ALL things without, which round about we see,
    We seek to know, and how therewith to do :
But that whereby we reason, live, and be,
    Within ourselves, we strangers are thereto.

We seek to know the moving of each sphere,
    And the strange cause of th' ebbs and floods of Nile ;
But of that clock within our breast we bear,
    The subtile motions we forget the while.

We that acquaint ourselves with every zone,
    And pass both tropics, and behold both poles,
When we come home are to ourselves unknown,
    And unacquainted still with our own souls.

We study speech, but others we persuade;
We leech-craft learn, but others cure with it;
We interpret laws which other men have made,
But read not those which in our hearts are writ.

It is because the mind is like the eye,
Through which it gathers knowledge by degrees,
Whose rays reflect not, but spread outwardly;
Not seeing itself when other things it sees.

E'en so man's soul which did God's image bear,
    And was at first fair, good, and spotless pure,
Since with her sins her beauties blotted were,
    Doth of all sights her own sight least endure.

For e'en at first reflection she espies
    Such strange chimeras and such monsters there,
Such toys, such antics, and such vanities,
    As she retires, and shrinks for shame and fear.

And as the man loves least at home to be
    That hath a sluttish house haunted with sprites;
So she impatient her own faults to see,
    Turns from herself and in strange things delights.

MAN'S GREATNESS AND MISERY.

I know my body's of so frail a kind,
    As force without, fevers within can kill:
I know the heavenly nature of my mind,
    But 'tis corrupted both in wit and will.

I know my soul hath power to know all things,
    Yet is she blind and ignorant in all:
I know I'm one of Nature's little kings,
    Yet to the least and vilest things am thrall.

I know my life's a pain and but a span;
    I know my sense is mocked in everything;
And, to conclude, I know myself a man,
    Which is a proud and yet a wretched thing.

THE SOUL'S TRUE SATISFACTION ONLY FOUND IN GOD.

As a king's daughter, being in person sought
    Of divers princes, who do neighbour near,
On none of them can fix a constant thought,
    Though she to all doth lend a gentle ear:

Yet she can love a foreign emperor,
    Whom of great worth and power she hears to be,
If she be woo'd but by ambassador,
    Or but his pictures or his letters see:

For well she knows, that when she shall be brought
    Into the kingdom where her spouse doth reign,
Her eyes shall see what she conceived in thought,
    Himself, his state, his glory, and his train:

So while the virgin soul on earth doth stay,
    She's wooed and tempted in ten thousand ways
By these great powers, which on the earth bear sway,
    The wisdom of the world, wealth, pleasure, praise.

With these sometimes she doth her time beguile,
    These do by fits her phantasy possess;
But she distastes them all within awhile,
    And in the sweetest finds a tediousness.

But if upon the world's Almighty King,
    She once doth fix her humble, loving thought,
Who by his picture drawn in everything,
    And sacred messages, her love hath sought;

Of Him she thinks she cannot think too much;
    This honey tasted still is ever sweet;
The pleasure of her ravished thought is such,
    As almost here she with her bliss doth meet:

But when in heaven she shall his essence see,
    This is her sovereign good, and perfect bliss:
Her longing, wishes, hopes, all finished be;
    Her joys are full, her motions rest in this:

There is she crowned with garlands of content;
    There doth she manna eat, and nectar drink:
That presence doth such high delights present,
    As never tongue could speak, nor heart could think.

THE CONCLUSION.

O ignorant, poor man! what dost thou bear,
    Locked up within the casket of thy breast!
What jewels, and what riches hast thou there!
    What heavenly treasure in so weak a chest!

Look in thy soul, and thou shalt beauties find,
    Like those which drowned Narcissus in the flood:
Honour and pleasure both are in thy mind,
    And all that in the world is counted good.

Think of her worth, and think that God did mean
    This worthy mind should worthy things embrace;
Blot not her beauties with thy thoughts unclean,
    Nor her dishonour with thy passion base.

Kill not her quickening power with surfeitings :
Mar not her sense with sensuality :
Cast not her serious wit on idle things :
Make not her free will slave to vanity.

And when thou think'st of her eternity,
Think not that death against her nature is ;
Think it a birth : and when thou go'st to die,
Sing like a swan, as if thou went'st to bliss.

And if thou, like a child, didst fear before,
Being in the dark, where thou didst nothing see ;
Now I have brought thee torch-light, fear no more ;
Now when thou diest, thou canst not hoodwinked be.

And thou, my soul, which turn'st with curious eye,
To view the beams of thine own form divine ;
Know that thou canst know nothing perfectly,
While thou art clouded with this flesh of mine.

Take heed of overweening, and compare
Thy peacock's feet with thy gay peacock's train ;
Study the best and highest things that are,
But of thyself a humble thought retain.

Cast down thyself, and only strive to raise
The glory of thy Maker's sacred name :
Use all thy powers that blessèd Power to praise,
Which gives thee power to be, and use the same.

SIR HENRY WOTTON.

BORN A.D. 1568; DIED A.D. 1639.

WOTTON was born at Boughton Hall, in Kent, and educated at Winchester and Queen's College, Oxford. After spending some years abroad, he became secretary to the Earl of Essex, whom he accompanied in his campaigns against the Spaniards and the Irish rebels On the fall of his patron, he retired to Florence, where he rendered important services to James VI. of Scotland. On the accession of James to the crown of England, Wotton received the honour of knighthood, and was appointed ambassador to the Republic of Venice. Having served his country in various embassies to different Continental courts, he was, in 1622, made Provost of Eton College, when he took holy orders. The remainder of his life was spent in the study of the Scriptures and the exercises of devotion. His biography was written by Isaac Walton.

"A HYMN TO MY GOD IN A NIGHT OF MY LATE SICKNESS."

O THOU great Power! in whom I move,
  For whom I live, to whom I die,
Behold me through Thy beams of love,
  Whilst on this couch of tears I lie;
    And cleanse my sordid soul within
    By Thy Christ's blood, the bath of sin.

No hallow'd oils, no gums I need,
  No rag of saints, no purging fire;
One rosy drop from David's seed
  Was worlds of seas to quench Thine ire.
    O Precious Ransom! which, once paid,
    That *consummatum est*[1] was said;

---

[1] "It is finished."

And said by Him, who said no more,
    But seal'd it with His dying breath.
Thou, then, that hast dispunged[1] my score,
    And dying wast the death of Death,
Be to me, (now on Thee I call,)
My life, my strength, my joy, my all.

THE CHARACTER OF A HAPPY LIFE.

How happy is he born and taught,
    That serveth not another's will;
Whose armour is his honest thought,
    And simple truth his utmost skill!

Whose passions not his masters are,
    Whose soul is still prepared for death,
Untied unto the worldly care
    Of public fame or private breath;

Who envies none that chance doth raise,
    Or vice : who never understood
How deepest wounds are given by praise :
    Nor rules of state, but rules of good :

Who hath his life from rumours freed,
    Whose conscience is his strong retreat ;
Whose state can neither flatterers feed,
    Nor ruin make oppressors great :

[1] Cleared off.

Who God doth late and early pray,
  More of his grace than gifts to lend;
And entertains the harmless day
  With a religious book or friend.

This man is freed from servile bands
  Of hope to rise, or fear to fall;
Lord of himself, though not of lands,
  And having nothing yet hath all.

"HYMN MADE BY SIR H. WOTTON WHEN HE WAS AN AMBASSADOR AT VENICE IN THE TIME OF THE GREAT SICKNESS THERE."

ETERNAL Mover! whose diffusèd glory,
  To show our grovelling reason what Thou art,
Unfolds itself in clouds of Nature's story,
  Where man, Thy proudest creature, acts his part :
Whom yet, alas! I know not why, we call
The world's contracted sum, the little all.

For what are we but lumps of walking clay?
  Why should we swell? Why should our spirits rise?
Are not brute beasts as strong, and birds as gay,
  Trees longer lived, and creeping things as wise?
Only our soul was left an inward light
To feel our weakness, and confess Thy might.

VENICE.

Thou then, our strength, Father of life and death,
  To whom our thanks, our vows, ourselves we owe,
From me, Thy tenant of this fading breath,
  Accept these lines which from Thy goodness flow :
And Thou that wert Thy royal prophet's muse,
Do not Thy praise in weaker strains refuse.

Let these poor notes ascend unto Thy throne,
  Where majesty doth sit, with mercy crowned :
Where my Redeemer lives, in whom alone

The errors of my wandering life are drowned;
Where all the quire of heaven resound the same,
That only Thine, Thine is the saving name.

Well then, my soul, joy in the midst of pain;
    Thy Christ that conquered hell, shall from above
With greater triumph yet return again,
    And conquer His own justice with His love;
Commanding earth and seas to render those
Unto His bliss, for whom He paid His woes.

Now have I done, now are my thoughts at peace,
    And now my joys are stronger than my grief;
I feel those comforts that shall never cease,
    Future in hope, but present in belief:
Thy words are true, Thy promises are just,
And Thou wilt find Thy dearly-bought, in dust.

BEMERTON CHURCH.

GEORGE HERBERT.

BORN A. D. 1593; DIED A. D. 1632.

GEORGE HERBERT was born at Montgomery Castle on April 3, 1593. He belonged to a branch of the family of the earls of Pembroke. He lost his father when he was four years old, and was brought up under the watchful care of a pious mother. Having been sent by her to Westminster School, he was from it elected a scholar of Trinity College, Cambridge, of which he afterwards became a fellow. In 1619, he was chosen orator of the University. The duties of this office brought him into connexion with King James I. who entertained the highest opinion of his learning and wisdom, and delighted to have him at court. He seemed thus to be in the way for high preferment. But on the death of the King, he retired from court, and, after much solemn consideration, determined to give up the brilliant prospect before him, and to enter the ministry. The spirit in which his resolution was formed may be seen in his answer to a friend, who wished to dissuade him from entering on a course of life which he thought unworthy of his birth and talents: "Though," he says, "the iniquity of the late times have made clergymen meanly valued, and the sacred name of priest contemptible, yet I will labour to make it honourable, by consecrating all my learning, and all my poor abilities, to advance the glory of that God that gave them; knowing that I can never do too much for Him that hath done so much for me, as to make me a Christian. And I will labour to be like my Saviour—by making humility lovely in the minds of all men, and by following the merciful and meek example of my dear Jesus."

In 1626, he was made prebend of the church of Leighton, in Bedfordshire. The edifice was in a ruinous condition, and he rebuilt it at his own cost, aided by contributions which he obtained from his friends. In the year 1630, he married, and

SALISBURY FROM THE PATH TO BEMERTON.

three months after was appointed to the rectory of Bemerton, near Salisbury. Here for the remaining two years of his life he laboured as a devoted servant of Christ, diligently discharging all those duties which he has so beautifully set forth in his "Country Parson." His character, in its simplicity and holiness, is vividly depicted in the pages of Isaac Walton, who describes the earnestness of his preaching, the fidelity of his catechising, his kindly intercourse with his parishioners, his faithful dealing with them in private conversation, the spirit of devout prayerfulness in which his work was carried on, his sympathy with those in trouble, and his self-denying charity. His chief recreation was music, and twice a week he used to walk over to Salisbury to join in the cathedral service, and take part in a private musical meeting. Many of his hymns were set to music by himself. He died in perfect peace, after commending his soul to the Saviour whom he loved, in the thirty-ninth year of his age, 1632. He had, on his death-bed, been reminded by a friend of his rebuilding Leighton Church, and many other acts of liberality in the service of his Master; but he answered: "They be good deeds if they be sprinkled with the blood of Christ, and not otherwise."

His poems are chiefly contained in his work called "The Temple." Like those of his contemporaries they contain quaint expressions, figures, and illustrations which are not suited to modern taste. But we forget these, in the true spirit of poetry which breathes through them, and above all in the holy fervour and humble devotion which pervades every part. Even those who do not altogether sympathize with his ecclesiastical views and tendencies cannot fail to see that he valued the outward form for the sake of the inner reality, and that the foundation of his religion was a devotion of heart and life to his Divine Master and Saviour whom he loved with all the ardent attachment of a personal friend. When only sixteen years of age, he wrote to his mother, sending her some sonnets he had composed: "My meaning, dear mother, is in these sonnets to declare my resolution to be, that my poor abilities in poetry shall be all and ever consecrated to God's glory." Well, indeed, was he enabled to carry out his resolution.

DIVINE WORSHIP.

When once thy foot enters the church, be bare.
God is more there than thou: for thou art there
Only by His permission. Then beware,
And make thyself all reverence and fear.
 Kneeling ne'er spoil'd silk stocking: quit thy state:
 All equal are within the church's gate.

Resort to sermons, but to prayers most:
Praying 's the end of preaching. Oh be drest;
Stay not for th' other pin. Why, thou hast lost
A joy for it worth worlds. Thus hell doth jest
 Away thy blessings, and extremely flout thee,
 Thy clothes being fast, but thy soul loose about thee.

In time of service, seal up both thine eyes,
And send them to thy heart; that, spying sin,
They may weep out the stains by them did rise.
Those doors being shut, all by the ear comes in.
  Who marks in church-time others' symmetry,
  Makes all their beauty his deformity.

Let vain or busy thoughts have there no part;
Bring not thy plough, thy plots, thy pleasure thither.
Christ purged His temple; so must thou thy heart.
All worldly thoughts are but thieves met together
  To cozen thee. Look to thy actions well,
  For churches either are our heaven or hell.

Judge not the preacher; for he is thy judge:
If thou mislike him, thou conceiv'st him not.
God calleth preaching folly. Do not grudge
To pick out treasures from an earthen pot.
  The worst speak something good: if all want sense,
  God takes a text, and preacheth patiè128nce.

He that gets patience, and the blessing which
Preachers conclude with, hath not lost his pains.
He that by being at church escapes the ditch
Which he might fall in by companions, gains.
  He that loves God's abode, and to combine
  With saints on earth, shall one day with them shine.

Jest not at preacher's language or expression:
How know'st thou, but thy sins made him miscarry?
Then turn thy faults and his into confession:
God sent him, whatsoe'er he be: oh tarry,

And love him for his Master: his condition,
Though it be ill, makes him no ill physician.

None shall in hell such bitter pangs endure
As those, who mock at God's way of salvation.
Whom oil and balsams kill, what salve can cure?
They drink with greediness a full damnation.
　　The Jews refusèd thunder; and we, folly.
　　Though God do hedge us in, yet who is holy?

Sum up at night what thou hast done by day;
And in the morning, what thou hast to do.
Dress and undress thy soul: mark the decay
And growth of it: if with thy watch, that too
　　Be down, then wind up both; since we shall be
　　Most surely judged, make thy accounts agree.

In brief, acquit thee bravely; play the man:
Look not on pleasures as they come, but go.
Defer not the least virtue: life's poor span
Make not an ell, by trifling in thy woe.
　　If thou do ill, the joy fades, not the pains:
　　If well, the pain doth fade, the joy remains.

SIN.

LORD, with what care hast Thou begirt us round:
　　Parents first season us; then schoolmasters
Deliver us to laws; they send us bound
　　To rules of reason, holy messengers,

Pulpits and Sundays, sorrow dogging sin,
   Afflictions sorted, anguish of all sizes,
Fine nets and stratagems to catch us in,
   Bibles laid open, millions of surprises,
Blessings beforehand, ties of gratefulness,
   The sound of glory ringing in our ears;
Without, our shame; within, our consciences;
   Angels and grace, eternal hopes and fears.

Yet all these fences and their whole array
One cunning bosom-sin blows quite away!

PEACE.

SWEET Peace, where dost thou dwell? I humbly crave
      Let me once know.
   I sought thee in a secret cave,
      And asked if Peace was there.
A hollow wind did seem to answer, No:
      Go seek elsewhere.

I did: and, going, did a rainbow note:
      Surely, thought I,
   This is the lace of Peace's coat:
      I will search out the matter.
But while I looked, the clouds immediately
      Did break and scatter.

Then went I to a garden, and did spy
      A gallant flower,

The crown imperial. Sure, said I,
    Peace at the root must dwell.
But when I digg'd, I saw a worm devour
    What showed so well.

At length I met a reverend good old man,
    Whom when for Peace
    I did demand, he thus began :
    There was a Prince of old
At Salem dwelt, who lived with good increase
    Of flock and fold.

He sweetly lived; yet sweetness did not save
    His life from foes.
But after death, out of his grave
    There sprang twelve stalks of wheat :
Which many wondering at, got some of those
    To plant and set.

It prospered strangely, and did soon disperse
    Through all the earth :
For they that taste it do rehearse,
    That virtue lies therein ;
A secret virtue, bringing peace and mirth
    By flight of sin.

Take of this grain which in my garden grows,
    And grows for you :
    Make bread of it; and that repose
    And peace which everywhere
With so much earnestness you do pursue
    Is only there.

GRACE.

My stock lies dead, and no increase
  Doth my dull husbandry improve;
Oh let Thy graces without cease
    Drop from above!

If still the sun should hide his face,
  Thy house would but a dungeon prove;
Thy works, night's captives: oh let grace
    Drop from above!

The dew doth every morning fall;
  And shall the dew outstrip Thy Dove?
The dew, for which grass cannot call,
    Drop from above?

Death is still working like a mole,
  And digs my grave at each remove:
Let grace work too, and on my soul
    Drop from above.

Sin is still hammering my heart
  Unto a hardness void of love;
Let suppling grace, to cross his art,
    Drop from above.

Oh come! for Thou dost know the way:
  Or if to me Thou wilt not move,
Remove me where I need not say—
    Drop from above.

PARADISE.

This piece is inserted as affording a good example of the quaint conceits which
Herbert so often delighted to employ.

I BLESS Thee, Lord, because I GROW
Among Thy trees, which in a ROW
To Thee both fruit and order OW.

What open force or hidden CHARM
Can blast my fruit or bring me HARM,
When the inclosure is Thine ARM ?

When Thou dost greater judgments SPARE,
And with Thy knife but prune and PARE,
E'en fruitful trees more fruitful ARE.

Such sharpness shows the sweetest FRIEND :
Such cuttings rather heal than REND :
And such beginnings touch their END.

THE CALL.

COME, my Way, my Truth, my Life !
Such a way, as gives us breath :
Such a truth, as ends all strife :
Such a life, as killeth death.

Come, my Light, my Feast, my Strength!
Such a light, as shows a feast:
Such a feast, as mends in length:
Such a strength, as makes his guest.

Come, my Joy, my Love, my Heart!
Such a joy, as none can move:
Such a love, as none can part:
Such a heart, as joys in love.

THE QUIP.

THE merry world did, on a day,
   With his train-bands and mates agree
To meet together where I lay,
   And all in sport to jeer at me.

First, Beauty crept into a rose;
   Which when I plucked not, Sir, said she,
Tell me, I pray, whose hands are those?
   But Thou shalt answer, Lord, for me.

Then Money came; and, chinking still,
   What tune is this, poor man? said he,
I heard in music you had skill:
   But Thou shalt answer, Lord, for me.

Then came brave Glory puffing by,
   In silks that whistled, who but he!
He scarce allowed me half an eye:
   But Thou shalt answer, Lord, for me.

Then came quick Wit and Conversation,
  And he would needs a comfort be;
And, to be short, make an oration:
  But Thou shalt answer, Lord, for me.

Yet when the hour of Thy design
  To answer these fine things shall come,
Speak not at large; say, I am Thine:
  And then they have their answer home.

LOVE.

Love bade me welcome; yet my soul drew back,
  Guilty of dust and sin;
But quick-eyed Love, observing me grow slack
  From my first entrance in,
Drew nearer to me, sweetly questioning,
  If I lacked anything.

A guest, I answered, worthy to be here.
  Love said, You shall be he.
I, the unkind, ungrateful? Ah, my dear,
  I cannot look on thee.
Love took my hand, and smiling did reply,—
  Who made the eyes but I?

Truth, Lord, but I have marred them: let my shame
  Go where it doth deserve.
And know you not, says Love, who bore the blame?
  My dear, then I will serve.
You must sit down, says Love, and taste my meat:
  So I did sit and eat.

SUNDAY.

The Sunday before his death (says Isaac Walton), he rose suddenly from his bed or couch, called for one of his instruments, took it into his hand, and said,

'My God, my God,
My music shall find Thee,
And every string
Shall have his attribute to sing.'

And having tuned it, he played and sang 'The Sundays of Man's Life,'

O DAY most calm, most bright,
The fruit of this, the next world's bud,
Th' endorsement of supreme delight,
Writ by a Friend, and with his blood;
The couch of time; care's balm and bay;
The week were dark, but for thy light:
Thy torch doth show the way.

The other days and thou
Make up one man; whose face *thou* art,
Knocking at heaven with thy brow:
The working days are the back part;
The burden of the week lies there,
Making the whole to stoop and bow,
Till thy release appear.

Man had straight forward gone
To endless death; but thou dost pull
And turn us round to look on One,
Whom, if we were not very dull,
We could not choose but look on still;
Since there is no place so alone
The which he doth not fill.

"O DAY MOST CALM, MOST BRIGHT."

Sundays the pillars are,
On which Heaven's palace archèd lies:
The other days fill up the spare
And hollow room with vanities.
They are the fruitful beds and borders
Of God's rich garden: that is bare
    Which parts their ranks and orders.

The Sundays of man's life,
Threaded together on Time's string,
Make bracelets to adorn the wife
Of the eternal glorious King.
On Sunday heaven's gate stands ope;
Blessings are plentiful and rife,
    More plentiful than hope.

This day my Saviour rose,
And did enclose this light for His,
That, as each beast its manger knows,
Man might not of his fodder miss.
Christ hath took in this piece of ground,
And made a garden there for those
    Who want herbs for their wound.

The rest of our creation
Our great Redeemer did remove
With the same shake which, at His passion,
Did th' earth and all things with it move.
As Samson bore the doors away,
Christ's hands, though nail'd, wrought our salvation,
    And did unhinge that day.

The brightness of that day
We sullied by our foul offence :
Wherefore that robe we cast away,
Having a new at His expense,
Whose drops of blood paid the full price
That was required to make us gay,
   And fit for Paradise.

Thou art a day of mirth :
And where the week-days trail on ground,
Thy flight is higher, as thy birth :
Oh let me take thee at the bound,
Leaping with thee from seven to seven,
Till that we both, being toss'd from earth,
   Fly hand in hand to heaven !

OLD ST. PAUL'S

J. DONNE, D.D.

BORN A.D. 1573; DIED A.D. 1631.

DR. DONNE was a native of the city of London, and studied at both Oxford and Cambridge. Being a Roman Catholic, however, he took no degree; but soon afterwards he renounced the errors of Romanism, after a careful study of the points of controversy. In the year 1601, he was offered preferment if he would take orders, but declined, lest the irregularities of his early life should be remembered against him, and bring dishonour on the sacred office of the ministry. These scruples were subsequently removed, and he was ordained in the year 1614. He became in succession, Lecturer at Lincoln's Inn, Dean of St. Paul's, and Rector of St. Dunstan's-in-the-West. He died A.D. 1631. Isaac Walton was his friend and biographer. His poems were much admired in his own time, but their rough versification, obscurity, and strange conceits, are little adapted to modern taste. The following short extracts will sufficiently illustrate their character.

"HYMN TO GOD, MY GOD, IN MY SICKNESS."

We think that Paradise and Calvary,
  Christ's cross and Adam's tree, stood in one place :[1]
Look, Lord, and find both Adams met in me;
  As the first Adam's sweat surrounds my face,
  May the last Adam's blood my soul embrace.

So in His purple wrapped, receive me, Lord,
  By these His thorns give me His other crown;
And as to others' souls I preached Thy Word,
  Be this my text, my sermon to mine own:
  Therefore that He may raise, the Lord throws down.

THE DAY OF JUDGMENT.

At the round earth's imagined corners blow
Your trumpets, angels; and arise, arise
From death, you numberless infinities
Of souls, and to your scattered bodies go:
All whom the flood did, and fire shall o'erthrow,
All whom war, death, age, ague's tyrannies,
Despair, law, chance hath slain; and you, whose eyes
Shall behold God, and never taste death's woe.

[1] Referring to an old tradition that the cross stood on the spot where Adam was buried.

But let them sleep, Lord, and me mourn a space;
For if above all these my sins abound,
'Tis late to ask abundance of Thy grace
When we are there. Here on this holy ground
Teach me how to repent; for that's as good
As if Thou'dst sealed my pardon with Thy blood.[1]
Sonnet VII. Divine Poems.

FROM "THE LITANY."

Hear us, O hear us, Lord: to Thee
   A sinner is more music, when he prays,
   Than spheres' or angels' praises be
      In panegyric hallelujahs;
      Hear us; for till Thou hear us, Lord,
   We know not what to say:
Thine ear to sighs, tears, thoughts, gives voice and word.
   O Thou, who Satan heard'st in Job's sick day,
   Hear Thyself now, for Thou, in us, dost pray.

That we may change to evenness,
   This intermitting, aguish piety,
That snatching cramps of wickedness,
   And apoplexies of fast sin may die;
      That music of Thy promises,
      Not threats in thunder, may
Awaken us to our just offices;
   What in Thy book Thou dost, or creatures, say,
   That we may hear, Lord, hear us when we pray.

---

[1] What Donne means in this obscure passage is that he to whom God gives the grace of true repentance, will surely enjoy forgiveness and all the blessings of the gospel.

EXETER CATHEDRAL.

JOSEPH HALL, D.D.

BORN A.D. 1574; DIED A.D. 1656.

THE author of the well-known "Contemplations" was born at Ashby-de-la-Zouch, and from the school in that town he passed to Emmanuel College, Cambridge. He accepted, but speedily resigned, the mastership of Tiverton School. Having become rector of Halstead, he soon rose to eminence, and in 1607, was made chaplain to Henry, Prince of Wales. In the year 1617, he became Dean of Worcester. He appeared as one of the representatives of the Church of England, at the Synod of Dort in 1618. In 1627, he was made bishop of Exeter, and at that time was looked upon with suspicion as a favourer of the Puritans. In 1641, he was translated to Norwich, and in the same year was imprisoned in the Tower, for protesting, with other bishops, against laws made while they were excluded from Parliament. He was expelled from his see in the year 1643, and retired to Higham, near Norwich, where he lived unmolested till his death in 1656.

In his youth he published some poetical satires, which Milton derided as "toothless," and which now are scarcely remembered; but his name lives, and is honoured as that of a devoted Christian minister, who, in his theological writings, has left behind him stores of plain, thoughtful, and forcible expositions of Scriptural truth, which are still read and valued by multitudes.

ANTHEMS FOR THE CATHEDRAL OF EXETER.

I.

LORD, what am I? A worm, dust, vapour, nothing!
What is my life? A dream, a daily dying!
What is my flesh? My soul's uneasy clothing!
What is my time? A minute ever flying!
 My time, my flesh, my life, and I,
 What are we, Lord, but vanity?

Where am I, Lord? Down in a vale of death.
What is my trade? Sin, my dear God offending.
My sport, sin too! My stay, a puff of breath.
What end of sin? Hell's horror never ending.
 My way, my trade, sport, stay, and place,
 Help to make up my doleful case.

Lord, what art Thou? Pure life, power, beauty, bliss.
Where dwell'st Thou? Up above in perfect light.
What is Thy time? Eternity it is.
What state? Attendance of each glorious sprite.
 Thyself, Thy place, Thy days, Thy state,
 Pass all the thoughts of powers create.

How shall I reach Thee, Lord? Oh, soar above,
Ambitious soul: but which way should I fly?
Thou, Lord, art way and end. What wings have I?
Aspiring thoughts of faith, of hope, of love:
    Oh, let these wings, that way alone,
    Present me to Thy blissful throne.

II.

LEAVE, O my soul, this baser world below,
Oh, leave this doleful dungèon of woe,
And soar aloft to that supernal rest
That maketh all the saints and angels blest:
    Lo, there the Godhead's glorious throne,
    Like to ten thousand suns in one!

Lo, there thy Saviour dear, in glory dight,
Adored of all the powers of heaven bright:
Lo, there that head, that bled with thorny wound,
Shines ever with celestial honour crowned:
    That hand that held the scornful reed
    Makes all the fiends infernal dread.

That back and side that ran with bloody streams,
Daunt angels' eyes with their majestic beams;
Those feet, once fastened to the cursèd tree,
Trample on Death and Hell in glorious glee;
    Those lips, once drenched with gall, do make
    With their dread doom the world to quake.

Behold those joys thou never canst behold;
Those precious gates of pearl, those streets of gold,
Those streams of life, those trees of Paradise
That never can be seen by mortal eyes:
    And when thou seest this state divine,
    Think that it is, or shall be thine.

See there the happy troops of purest sprites;
That live above in endless true delights;
And see where once thyself shall rangèd be,
And look and long for immortality:
    And now beforehand help to sing
    Hallelujahs to heaven's King.

WILLIAM DRUMMOND.

BORN A.D. 1585; DIED A.D. 1649.

THIS poet is commonly known as "Drummond of Hawthornden," which place he inherited from his father, Sir John Drummond. He was educated at the High School and University of Edinburgh. His life was chiefly spent in foreign travel and in the pursuits of literature. Towards the close of it he was exposed to much trouble on account of his firm attachment to the royal cause; and grief for the death of Charles I. is said to have hastened his own, which took place, December 4, 1649.

ALL IS VANITY.

A GOOD that never satisfies the mind,
A beauty fading like the April showers,
A sweet with floods of gall that runs combined,
A pleasure passing ere, in thought, made ours,
An honour that more fickle is than wind,
A glory at opinion's frown that lowers,
A treasury which bankrupt time devours,
A knowledge than grave ignorance more blind,
A vain delight our equals to command,
A style of greatness in effect a dream,
A swelling thought of holding sea and land,
A servile lot decked with a pompous name :
Are the strange ends we toil for here below,
Till wisest death make us our errors know.

HYMN.

Saviour of mankind! Man Emmanuel!
Who sinless died for sin, who vanquished hell,
The first-fruits of the grave, whose life did give
Light to our darkness, in whose death we live
O strengthen Thou my faith, correct my will,
That mine may Thine obey: protect me still,
So that the latter death may not devour
My soul sealed with Thy seal; so in the hour
When Thou, whose body sanctified Thy tomb
(Unjustly judged), a glorious Judge, shalt come
To judge the world with justice; by that sign
I may be known and entertained for Thine.

HEAVENLY JERUSALEM.

HYMN FOR THE DEDICATION OF A CHURCH.

Jerusalem, that place divine,
   The vision of sweet peace is named;[1]
In heaven her glorious turrets shine,
   Her walls of living stones are framed;
     While angels guard her on each side,
     Fit company for such a bride.

She, decked in new attire, from heaven
   Her wedding chamber, now descends,
Prepared in marriage to be given
   To Christ, on whom her joy depends.
     Her walls, wherewith she is enclosed,
     And streets are of pure gold composed.

[1] The word 'Jerusalem' has been thought to mean the vision or home of peace.

The gates, adorned with pearls most bright,
  The way to hidden glory show;
And thither by the blessed might
  Of faith in Jesus' merits, go
    All those who are on earth distressed,
    Because they have Christ's name professed.

These stones the workmen dress and beat,
  Before they throughly polished are;
Then each is in his proper seat
  Established, by the Builder's care,
    In this fair frame to stand for ever,
    So joined that them no force can sever.

To God, who sits in highest seat,
  Glory and power given be;
To Father, Son, and Paraclete,
  Who reign in equal dignity;
    Whose boundless power we still adore,
    And sing their praise for evermore.

FRANCIS QUARLES.

BORN A.D. 1592; DIED A.D. 1644.

QUARLES was born near Romford, in Essex, A.D. 1592. He greatly distinguished himself at school by his progress in learning, and took his degree at Christ College, Cambridge, in his 16th year. He shortly afterwards entered as a student at Lincoln's Inn, but soon abandoned the study of the law, and was made cupbearer to Elizabeth, Queen of Bohemia, which office, however, he could have held for only a very short time, for in 1621, we find him in Ireland, where he became private secretary to Archbishop Usher. It is not exactly known when he returned to England, but in 1639, he was appointed Chronologer to the City of London, in which office he had the arrangement of the civic pageants. After suffering much trouble and loss from his attachment to the royal cause, he died in 1644, and was buried in the church of St. Vedast, Foster Lane.

He was a very voluminous writer. His most popular work was his "Emblems," first published in 1635. Each emblem was illustrated by a rough and generally grotesque woodcut; or, rather, the poetry was accommodated to and written for the cuts, which were already in existence. This work once enjoyed great popularity, though it is now comparatively little read. The occasional coarseness and bad taste by which his poetry is disfigured makes it distasteful to modern readers; but it contains much that is forcible and impressive, and the vanity of the world and the consolations of true religion are powerfully set forth.

JOB XIII. 24.

"Wherefore hidest Thou Thy face, and holdest me for Thine enemy."

[*Illustration.*—One seeking to remove an angel's hand, which is hiding the angel's face.]

WHY dost Thou shade Thy lovely face? Oh, why
Does that eclipsing hand so long deny
The sunshine of Thy soul-enliv'ning eye?

Without that light, what light remains in me?
Thou art my Life, my Way, my Light; in Thee
I live, I move, and by Thy beams I see.

Thou art my Life; if Thou but turn away,
My life's a thousand deaths. Thou art my Way;
Without Thee, Lord, I travel not, but stray.

My Light Thou art; without Thy glorious sight,
Mine eyes are darkened with perpetual night.
My God, Thou art my Way, my Life, my Light.

Thou art my Way; I wander if Thou fly:
Thou art my Light; if hid, how blind am I !
Thou art my Life; if Thou withdraw, I die.

Mine eyes are blind and dark, I cannot see;
To whom or whither should my darkness flee,
But to the light ? and who's that light but Thee ?

My path is lost, my wand'ring steps do stray;
I cannot safely go, nor safely stay;
Whom should I seek but Thee, my Path, my Way ?

If I have lost my path, great Shepherd, say,
Shall I still wander in a doubtful way ?
Lord, shall a lamb of Israel's sheepfold stray ?

Thou art the pilgrim's Path, the blind man's Eye,
The dead man's Life; on Thee my hopes rely:
If Thou remove, I err, I grope, I die.

Disclose Thy sunbeams, close Thy wings, and stay;
See, see how I am blind, and dead, and stray,
O Thou that art my Light, my Life, my Way.

'Emblems,' Book III. No. 7.

FLEEING FROM WRATH.

JOB XIV. 13.

"O that Thou wouldest hide me in the grave, that Thou wouldest keep me secret, until Thy wrath be past."

[*Illustration.*— One hiding in a cavern from an angry descending angel.]

Oh, whither shall I fly? what path untrod
Shall I seek out to 'scape the flaming rod
Of my offended, of my angry God?

Where shall I sojourn? What kind sea will hide
My head from thunder? Where shall I abide
Until His flames be quenched or laid aside?

What if my feet should take their hasty flight,
And seek protection in the shades of night?
Alas! no shades can blind the God of light.

What if my soul should take the wings of day
And find some desert? If she springs away,
The wings of vengeance clip as fast as they.

What if some solid rock should entertain
My frighted soul? can solid rocks restrain
The stroke of Justice, and not cleave in twain?

Nor sea, nor shade, nor shield, nor rock, nor cave,
Nor silent deserts, nor the sullen grave,
What flame-eyed Fury means to smite, can save.

The seas will part, graves open, rocks will split;
The shield will cleave; the frighted shadows flit;
Where Justice aims, her fiery darts must hit.

No, no, if stern-browed Vengeance means to thunder,
There is no place above, beneath, or under,
So close, but will unlock, or rive in sunder.

'Tis vain to flee; 'tis neither here nor there
Can 'scape that hand, until that hand forbear:
Ah me! where is He not, that's ev'rywhere?

'Tis vain to flee, till gentle Mercy show
Her better eye ; the farther off we go,
The swing of Justice deals the mightier blow.

The ingenuous child, corrected, doth not fly
His angry mother's hand ; but climbs more nigh,
And quenches with his tears her flaming eye.

Shadows are faithless, and the rocks are false ;
No trust in brass, no trust in marble walls ;
Poor cots are e'en as safe as princes' halls.

Great God ! there is no safety here below ;
Thou art my fortress, Thou that seem'st my foe,
'Tis Thou, that strik'st the stroke, must guard the blow.

Thou art my God ; by Thee I fall or stand ;
Thy grace hath given me courage to withstand
All tortures but my conscience and Thy hand.

I know Thy justice is Thyself ; I know,
Just God, Thy very self is mercy too :
If not to Thee, where, whither should I go ?

Then work Thy will ; if passion bid me flee,
My reason shall obey ; my wings shall be
Stretched out no further than from Thee to Thee.

'Emblems,' Book III. No. 12.

PSALM LXXIII. 25.

"Whom have I in heaven but Thee? and there is none upon earth that I desire beside thee."

[*Illustration.*—One sitting on a globe, and looking up to heaven where God sits.]

I LOVE (and have some cause to love) the earth;
   She is my Maker's creature, therefore good;
She is my mother, for she gave me birth;
   She is my tender nurse, she gives me food.
But what's a creature, Lord, compared with Thee?
Or what's my mother, or my nurse to me?

I love the air; her dainty fruits refresh
   My drooping soul, and to new sweets invite me;
Her shrill mouth'd choirs sustain me with their flesh,
   And with their polyphonian notes delight me:
But what's the air, or all the sweets that she
Can bless my soul withal, compared to Thee?

I love the sea; she is my fellow-creature;
   My careful purveyor; she provides me store;
She walls me round; she makes my diet greater;
   She wafts my treasure from a foreign shore:
But, Lord of oceans, when compared with Thee,
What is the ocean, or her wealth to me?

To heav'n's high city I direct my journey,
   Whose spangled suburbs entertain mine eye;
Mine eye by contemplation's great attorney,
   Transcends the crystal pavement of the sky:
But what is heav'n, great God, compared to Thee?
Without Thy presence, heav'n's no heav'n to me.

Without Thy presence, earth gives no refection ;
Without Thy presence, sea affords no treasure ;
Without Thy presence, air's a rank infection ;
Without Thy presence, heav'n itself's no pleasure :
If not possess'd, if not enjoyed in Thee,
What's earth, or sea, or air, or heav'n to me ?

The highest honours that the world can boast
Are subjects far too low for my desire ;
Its brightest beams of glory are, at most,
But dying sparkles of Thy living fire :
The brightest flames that earth can kindle be
But nightly glow-worms, if compared to Thee.

Without Thy presence, wealth is bags of cares ;
Wisdom but folly ; joy, disquiet sadness ;
Friendship is treason, and delights are snares ;
Pleasure but pain, and mirth but pleasing madness :
Without Thee, Lord, things be not what they be,
Nor have their being, when compared with Thee.

In having all things, and not Thee, what have I ?
Not having Thee, what have my labours got ?
Let me enjoy but Thee, what farther crave I ?
And having Thee alone, what have I not ?
I wish nor sea, nor land ; nor would I be
Possess'd of heav'n, heav'n unpossess'd of Thee.

'Emblems,' Book V. No. 6.

ON JACOB'S PILLOW.

The bed was earth, the raisèd pillows stones,
Whereon poor Jacob rests his head, his bones;
Heaven was his canopy; the shades of night
Were his drawn curtains to exclude the light.
Poor state for Isaac's heir! It seems to me
His cattle found as soft a bed as he:
Yet God appearèd there, his joy, his crown;
God is not always seen in beds of down.
Oh if that God shall please to make my bed,
I care not where I rest my bones, my head:
With Thee my wants can never prove extreme—
With Jacob's pillow give me Jacob's dream.

'Divine Fancies,' I. 65.

THE LORD IS PITIFUL AND OF TENDER MERCY.

E'en as a nurse, whose child's imperfect pace
Can hardly lead his foot from place to place,
Leaves her fond kissing, sets him down to go,
Nor does uphold him for a step or two;
But when she finds that he begins to fall
She holds him up, and kisses him withal;—
So God from man sometimes withdraws His hand
Awhile, to teach his infant faith to stand;
But when He sees his feeble strength begin
To fail, He gently takes him up again.

'Job Militant.' Medit 2

TRUST IN GOD.

In Thee, dear Lord, my pensive soul respires;
Thou art the fulness of my choice desires;
Thou art that sacred spring, whose waters burst
In streams to him that seeks with holy thirst:
Thrice happy man, thrice happy thirst to bring
The fainting soul to so, so sweet a spring;
Thrice happy he, whose well-resolvèd breast
Expects no other aid, no other rest;
Thrice happy he, whose downy age hath been
Reclaimed by scourges from the prime of sin,
And, early seasoned with the taste of truth,
Remembers his Creator in his youth.
       'Sion's Elegies,' III. 9.

"WHAT PLEASANT GROVES, WHAT GOODLY FIELDS!
HOW FRUITFUL HILLS AND DALES HAVE WE!"

GEORGE WITHER,

BORN A.D. 1588; DIED A.D. 1667.

This writer was a native of Bentworth, near Alton, in Hampshire. He entered at Magdalen College, Oxford, but his course of study there was suddenly interrupted, and he returned home. Shortly afterwards, he came to London, and became a student at Lincoln's Inn. One of his earliest works as a writer was a satire upon the vices and follies of the time, called *Abuses Stript and Whipt*, the freedom and plainness of which gave great offence, and was the cause of his being committed to prison. During the civil wars he was at first a strong supporter of the Crown, but he subsequently became an ardent adherent of the Parliament, and fought on that side. At the Restoration he suffered imprisonment in the Tower, from which he was released in 1663. After living through the terrors of the Great Plague and Fire of London, he died in 1667, and was buried in the Church of the Savoy, in the Strand. The number of his sacred poems makes selection difficult; he wrote hymns for every imaginable circumstance and position in life. Though endowed with no great genius, yet his writings are marked by a simplicity and a Christian spirit, a purity and earnestness, which make him one of the most pleasing of our early Sacred Poets.

A PRAYER FOR ENGLAND.

It was Thy pleasure, Lord, to say
That whatsoever in Thy name
We prayed for, as we ought to pray,
Thou would'st vouchsafe to grant the same :
Oh, therefore we beseech Thee now,
To these our prayers which we make,
Thy gracious ear in favour bow,
And grant them for Thy mercy's sake.

Let not the seasons of the year,
As they their courses do observe,
Engender those contagions here,
Which our transgressions do deserve:
Let not the summer worms impair
Those bloomings of the earth we see :
Nor blastings, or distempered air,
Destroy those fruits that hopeful be.

Domestic brawls expel Thou far,
And be Thou pleased our coast to guard;
The dreadful sounds of in-brought war
Within our confines be not heard:
Continue also here Thy Word,
And make us thankful, we Thee pray,
The pestilence, dearth, and the sword,
Have been so long withheld away.

And as we heedfully observe
The certain limits of our grounds,
And, outward quiet to preserve,
About them walk our yearly rounds:
So let us also have a care
Our soul's possessions, Lord, to know,
That no encroachments on us there,
Be gainèd by our subtle foe.

What pleasant groves, what goodly fields!
How fruitful hills and dales have we!
How sweet an air our climate yields!
How stored with flocks and herds are we!
How milk and honey doth o'erflow!
How clear and wholesome are our springs!
How safe from ravenous beasts we go!
And oh, how free from poisonous things!

For these, and for our grass, our corn;
For all that springs from blade or bough;
For all those blessings that adorn,
Or wood, or field, this kingdom through:

For all of these, Thy praise we sing,
And humbly, Lord, entreat Thee too,
That fruit to Thee we forth may bring,
As unto us Thy creatures do.

So in the sweet refreshing shade
Of Thy protection sitting down,
The gracious favours we have had,
Relate we will to Thy renown;
Yea, other men, when we are gone,
Shall for Thy mercies honour Thee,
And famous make what Thou hast done
To such as after them shall be.

'Songs and Hymns of the Church,'
Hymn for Rogation Week.

HYMN FOR SUNDAY.

Six days, O Lord, the world to make,
And set all creatures in array,
Was all the leisure Thou would'st take,
And then didst rest the seventh day:
And rightly, by a law divine,
Which till the end of time shall last,
The seventh part of time is Thine.

Then teach us willingly to give
The tribute of our days to Thee;
By whom we now both move and live,
And have attained to what we be.

For of that rest, which by Thy word
Thou hast been pleasèd to enjoin,
The profit all is ours, O Lord,
And but the praise alone is Thine.

Oh, therefore let us not consent
To rob Thee of Thy Sabbath Day,
Nor rest with carnal rest content,
But sanctify it all we may:
Yea, grant that we from sinful strife,
And all those works Thou dost detest,
May keep a sabbath all our life,
And enter Thy eternal rest.

Ibid. Song 60.

A GENERAL INVITATION TO PRAISE GOD.

Come, O come, in pious lays,
Sound we God Almighty's praise;
Hither bring in one consent,
Heart, and voice, and instrument :
Music add of every kind,
Sound the trump, the cornet wind;
Strike the viol, touch the lute,
Let no tongue nor string be mute;
    Nor a creature dumb be found,
    That hath either voice or sound.

Let those things which do not live,
In still music praises give;
Lowly pipe, ye worms that creep
On the earth or in the deep:
Loud aloft your voices strain,
Beasts and monsters of the main ;
Birds, your warbling treble sing;
Clouds, your peals of thunder ring ;
 Sun and moon, exalted higher,
 And bright stars, augment this choir.

Come, ye sons of human race,
In this chorus take a place,
And, amid the mortal throng,
Be you masters of the song:
Angels and supernal powers,
Be the noblest tenor yours:
Let, in praise of God, the sound
Run a never-ending round ;
 That our song of praise may be
 Everlasting, as is He.

So from heaven on earth He shall
Let His gracious blessings fall ;
And this huge wide orb we see
Shall one choir, one temple, be ;
Where in such a praiseful tone,
We will sing what He hath done,
That the cursèd fiends below
Shall thereat impatient grow :
 Then, Oh come, in pious lays
 Sound we God Almighty's praise.
      'Hallelujah.' Hymn 1.

HYMN AT SUN-SETTING.

BEHOLD the sun, that seemed but now
    Enthronèd overhead,
Beginneth to decline below
    This globe whereon we tread;
And he whom yet we look upon
    With comfort and delight,
Will quite depart from hence, anon,
    And leave us to the night.

Thus time, unheeded, steals away
    The life which nature gave;
Thus are our bodies every day
    Declining to the grave.
Thus from us all those pleasures fly
    Whereon we set our heart;
And when the night of death draws nigh,
    Thus will they all depart.

Lord! though the sun forsake our sight,
    And mortal hopes are vain;
Let still Thine everlasting light
    Within our souls remain:
And in the nights of our distress,
    Vouchsafe those rays divine
Which from the Sun of righteousness
    For ever brightly shine.

A HYMN FOR A WIDOWER OR A WIDOW.

THE voice which I did more esteem
  Than Music in her sweetest key,
Those eyes which unto me did seem
  More comfortable than the day,
    These now by me as they have been,
    Shall never more be heard or seen ;
  But what I once enjoyed in them
  Shall seem hereafter as a dream.

All earthly comforts vanish thus,
  So little hold of them have we,
That we from them or they from us
  May in a moment ravished be ;
    Yet we are neither just nor wise,
    If present mercies we despise,
  Or mind not how there may be made
  A thankful use of what we had.

I therefore do not so bemoan,
  Though these beseeming tears I drop,
The loss of my belovèd one,
  As they that are deprived of hope ;
    But, in expressing of my grief,
    My heart receiveth some relief,
  And joyeth in the good I had,
  Although my sweets are bitter made.

Lord! keep me faithful to the trust
Which my dear spouse reposed in me,
To him now dead preserve me just
In all that should performèd be;
For though our being man and wife
Extendeth only to this life,
Yet neither life nor death should end
The being of a faithful friend.
'Hallelujah,' Part III. Hymn 27.

THE FIRST MARTYR.

LORD, with what zeal did Thy first Martyr breathe
Thy blessed truth, to such as him withstood!
With what stout mind embracèd he his death!
A holy witness sealing with his blood!
The praise is Thine, that him so strong didst make,
And blest is he, that dièd for Thy sake.

Unquenchèd love in him appeared to be,
When for his murderous foes he did intreat:
A piercing eye made bright by faith had he,
For he beheld Thee in Thy glory set;
And so unmoved his patience he did keep,
He died, as if he had but fall'n asleep.

Our lukewarm hearts with his hot zeal inflame,
So constant and so loving let us be;
So let us, living, glorify Thy name;
So let us, dying, fix our eyes on Thee:
And when the sleep of death shall us o'ertake,
With him, to life eternal, us awake.
Hymn for St. Stephen's Day.

HENRY KING, D.D.

BORN A.D. 1591; DIED A.D. 1669.

HENRY KING was the son of Dr. John King, Bishop of London. He was in succession appointed Prebend of St. Paul's, Archdeacon of Colchester, and Dean of Rochester. In 1641, he became Bishop of Chichester; but, in the following year, Chichester was besieged and taken by the Parliamentary forces, and the bishop was made prisoner. He lived in retirement till the Restoration, when he was recalled to his see, and died, 1669.

His poetical fame rests chiefly on the touching elegy in which he has recorded his grief and desolation on the loss of his beloved wife; but this poem cannot be considered to fall within the compass of the present work. The three brief pieces which follow will suffice to illustrate the real power and beauty of many of his thoughts.

SIC VITA.

LIKE to the falling of a star,
Or as the flights of eagles are,
Or like the fresh spring's gaudy hue,
Or silver drops of morning dew,
Or like a wind that chafes the flood,
Or bubbles which on water stood:
E'en such is man, whose borrow'd light
Is straight call'd in, and paid to-night.
  The wind blows out; the bubble dies;
  The spring entomb'd in autumn lies;
  The dew dries up; the star is shot;
  The flight is past—and man forgot.

HENRY KING, D.D.

MY MIDNIGHT MEDITATION.

ILL-BUSIED Man! why shouldst thou take such care
To lengthen out thy life's short kalendar?
When every spectacle thou look'st upon
Presents and acts thy execution.
    Each drooping season and each flower doth cry,
    "Fool! as I fade and wither, thou must die."

The beating of thy pulse (when thou art well)
Is just the tolling of thy passing bell:
Night is thy hearse, whose sable canopy
Covers alike deceasèd day and thee.
    And all those weeping dews which nightly fall
    Are but the tears shed for thy funeral.

THE DIRGE.

WHAT is th' existence of man's life
But open war, or slumber'd strife;
Where sickness to his sense presents
The combat of the elements;
And never feels a perfect peace
Till Death's cold hand signs his release?

It is a storm—where the hot blood
Outvies in rage the boiling flood;

HENRY KING, D.D.

"IT IS A DIAL—WHICH POINTS OUT
THE SUN-SET, AS IT MOVES ABOUT."

And each loose passion of the mind
Is like a furious gust of wind,
Which beats his bark with many a wave,
Till he casts anchor in the grave.

It is a flower—which buds and grows,
And withers as the leaves disclose ;
Whose spring and fall faint seasons keep,
Like fits of waking before sleep ;
Then shrinks into that fatal mould
Where its first being was enroll'd.

It is a dream—whose seeming truth
Is moraliz'd in age and youth,
Where all the comforts he can share
As wandering as his fancies are ;
Till, in a mist of dark decay,
The dreamer vanish quite away.

It is a dial—which points out
The sun-set, as it moves about ;
And shadows out in lines of night
The subtle stages of Time's flight ;
Till all-obscuring earth hath laid
His body in perpetual shade.

It is a weary interlude—
Which doth short joys, long woes, include :
The world the stage, the prologue, tears,
The acts, vain hopes and varied fears ;
The scene shuts up with loss of breath,
And leaves no epilogue but death.

ROBERT HERRICK.

BORN A.D. 1591; DIED A.D. 1674.

ROBERT HERRICK was a native of London, educated at St. John's College, Cambridge, and presented by King Charles I. to the vicarage of Dean Prior, in Devonshire. During the Commonwealth he was obliged to leave his benefice, but returned to it at the Restoration, and died there in 1674.

It is sad to think that one who could write so sweetly and well as Herrick should have perverted and misused his gifts. Many of his writings are stained with impurity, and are utterly repugnant to the sacred office which he held. The following lines show that at least he knew and, in his better moments, mourned over his fault :—

> "For those my unbaptized rhymes,
> Writ in my wild, unhallowed times—
> For every sentence, clause, and word,
> That's not inlaid with Thee, my Lord,
> Forgive me, God, and blot each line
> Out of my book that is not Thine;
> But if, 'mongst all, Thou find'st here one
> Worthy Thy benediction,
> That one, of all the rest, shall be
> The glory of my work and me."

LITANY TO THE HOLY SPIRIT.

In the hour of my distress,
When temptations me oppress,
And when I my sins confess,
    Sweet Spirit, comfort me.

When I lie within my bed,
Sick at heart and sick at head,
And with doubts discomforted,
    Sweet Spirit, comfort me.

When the house doth sigh and weep,
And the world is drowned in sleep,
Yet mine eyes their watch do keep,
  Sweet Spirit, comfort me.

When the priest his last hath prayed,
And I nod to what is said,
'Cause my strength is now decayed,
  Sweet Spirit, comfort me.

When, God knows, I'm tossed about
Either with despair or doubt,
Yet, before the glass be out,
  Sweet Spirit, comfort me.

When the tapers now burn blue,
And the comforters are few,
And that number, more than true,
  Sweet Spirit, comfort me.

When the judgment is revealed,
And that open which was sealed;
When to Thee I have appealed,
  Sweet Spirit, comfort me.

THE SOUL.

When once the soul has lost her way,
Oh then how restless does she stray;
And having not her God for light,
How does she err in endless night!

TO MY SAVIOUR.

Night hath no wings to him that cannot sleep,
And time seems then not for to fly, but creep;
Just so it is with me, who, listening, pray
The wind to blow the tedious night away,
That I might see the cheerful peeping day.
Sick is my heart; O Saviour, do Thou please
To make my bed soft in my sicknesses;
Lighten my candle, so that I beneath,
Sleep not for ever in the vaults of death:
Let me Thy voice betimes i' the morning hear;
Call and I'll come, say Thou the when and where:
Draw me but first, and after Thee I'll run,
And make no stop until my race be done.

HENRY VAUGHAN.

BORN A.D. 1621; DIED A.D. 1695.

HENRY VAUGHAN was a native of Brecknockshire, and was known among his contemporaries as the "Silurist," from the classical name of that part of Wales. He entered Jesus College, Oxford, but left without taking a degree, owing to the troubles of the Civil War. He was an ardent supporter of the royal cause, but could not reconcile himself to taking up arms against his countrymen, and retired to his native county, where he spent a long and retired life in practice as a physician. About the year 1648, he was brought low by a severe illness, which led to a great change in his religious views. On his recovery, he published the "Silex Scintillans," a collection of poems, in which he poured forth the experience of his heart and his feelings of love to the Saviour who had become so dear to him. A second part was afterwards added to it. But his poems, full of beauties as they are, were not appreciated by his contemporaries. He lived for forty years longer without publishing anything, and died a peaceful death on April 23, 1695.

He was a great admirer of George Herbert, in whose poems he found a great source of comfort and instruction. He closely imitated him in style and manner, but he was no mere copyist, and in some instances rises higher than his master. The similarity between them was not a mere agreement in literary taste; it was a common love for and devotion to the same Saviour which drew so closely together the English clergyman and the Welsh physician.

MORNING.

When first thy eyes unveil, give thy soul leave
To do the like; our bodies but forerun
The spirit's duty; true hearts spread and heave
Unto their God, as flowers do to the sun:
Give Him thy first thoughts then, so shalt thou keep
Him company all day, and in Him sleep.

"SERVE GOD BEFORE THE WORLD."

Yet never sleep the sun up; prayer should
    Dawn with the day, there are set, awful hours
'Twixt Heaven and us; the manna was not good
    After sun-rising, for day sullies flowers.
Rise to prevent the sun; sleep doth sins glut,
And Heaven's gate opens when the world's is shut.

Walk with thy fellow-creatures; note the hush
And whisperings amongst them. Not a spring
Or leaf but hath his *morning* hymn; each bush
And oak doth know I AM—canst thou not sing !
Oh leave thy cares and follies! Go this way,
And thou art sure to prosper all the day.

Serve God before the world; let Him not go,
Until thou hast a blessing; then resign
The whole unto Him; and remember who
Prevail'd by wrestling ere the sun did shine.
Pour oil upon the stones;[1] weep for thy sin;
Then journey on, and have an eye to heav'n.

Mornings are mysteries: the first world's youth,
Man's resurrection, and the future's bud,
Shroud in their births: the Crown of life, light, truth,
Is styl'd their Star,[2] the stone, and hidden food.
Three blessings wait upon them, two of which
Should move; they make us holy, happy, rich.

When the world's up, and every swarm abroad,
Keep thou thy temper; mix not with each clay;
Dispatch necessities: life hath a load
Which must be carried on, and safely may.
Yet keep those cares *without* thee: let the heart
Be God's alone, and choose the better part.

---

[1] Genesis xxviii. 18. [2] Revelation xxii. 16

SUNDAYS.

Bright shadows of true rest! some shoots of bliss!
    Heaven once a week;
The next world's gladness prepossessed in this;
    A day to seek
Eternity in time; the steps by which
    We climb above all ages; lamps that light
Man through his heap of dark days; and the rich
    And full redemption of the whole week's flight:
The pulleys unto headlong man; time's bower;
    The narrow way;
Transplanted paradise; God's walking hour—
    The cool o' the day;
The creature's jubilee; God's parle with dust;
    Heaven here; man on those hills of myrrh and flowers;
Angels descending; the returns of trust;
    A gleam of glory after six days' showers;
The church's love-feasts; time's prerogative
    And interest
Deducted from the whole; the combs, and hive,
    And home of rest;
The milky-way chalked out with suns; a clue
    That guides through erring hours; and, in full story,
A taste of heaven on earth; the pledge and cue
    Of a full feast, and the out-courts of glory.

BEGGING.

King of mercy, King of love,
In whom I live, in whom I move,
Perfect what Thou hast begun;
Let no night put out this sun.

Grant I may, my chief desire,
Long for Thee, to Thee aspire.
Let my youth, my bloom of days,
Be my comfort and Thy praise;
That hereafter, when I look
O'er the sullied sinful book,
I may find Thy hand therein,
Wiping out my shame and sin.
Oh, it is Thy only art
To reduce a stubborn heart;
And since Thine is victory,
Strongholds should belong to Thee.
Lord, then take it, leave it not
Unto my dispose and lot;
But since I would have it mine,
O my God, let it be Thine.

LOVE AND DISCIPLINE.

Since in a land not barren still,
Because Thou dost Thy grace distil,
My lot is fall'n, blest be Thy will!

And since these biting frosts but kill
Some tares in me, which choke or spill [1]
That seed Thou sow'st, blest be Thy skill!

Blest be thy dew, and blest thy frost,
And happy I to be so crost,
And cured, by crosses, at Thy cost.

---

[1] To spoil or injure; it is often used in this sense by the Elizabethan poets.

The dew doth cheer what is distrest,
The frosts ill weeds nip and molest,
In both Thou work'st unto the best.

That while Thy several mercies plot,
And work on me, now cold now hot,
The work goes on and slacketh not.

For as Thy hand the weather steers,
So thrive I best 'twixt joys and tears,
And all the year have some green ears.

THE RAINBOW.[1]

STILL young and fine! but what is still in view
We slight as old and soil'd, though fresh and new;
How bright wert thou when Shem's admiring eye
Thy burnished, flaming arch did first descry;
When Zarah, Nahor, Haran, Abram, Lot,
The youthful world's grey fathers, in one knot,
Did, with intentive looks, watch every hour
For thy new light, and trembled at each shower!
When thou dost shine, darkness looks white and fair;
Storms turn to music, clouds to smiles and air;
Rain gently spends his honey-drops, and pours
Balm on the cleft earth, milk on grass and flowers.
Bright pledge of peace and sunshine, the sure tie
Of the Lord's hand, the object of His eye!
When I behold thee, though my light be dim,
Distant, and low, I can in thine see Him
Who looks upon thee from His glorious throne,
And minds the covenant betwixt all and One.

[1] Compare Campbell's lines on the same subject.

PEACE.

My soul, there is a country
    Afar beyond the stars,
Where stands a winged sentry
    All skilful in the wars:
There above noise and danger,
    Sweet Peace sits, crowned with smiles,
And One born in a manger
    Commands the beauteous files.
He is thy gracious Friend,
    And (O my soul, awake!)
Did in pure love descend,
    To die here for thy sake.
If thou canst get but thither,
    There grows the flower of peace,
The rose that cannot wither,
    Thy fortress, and thine ease.
Leave then thy foolish ranges;
    For none can thee secure,
But One who never changes,
    Thy God, thy Life, thy Cure.

DEPARTED FRIENDS.

They are all gone into a world of light,
    And I alone sit lingering here;
Their very memory is fair and bright,
    And my sad thoughts doth clear.

It glows and glitters in my cloudy breast,
    Like stars upon some gloomy grove;
Or those faint beams in which the hill is drest
    After the sun's remove.

I see them walking in an air of glory,
    Whose light doth trample on my days;
My days which are at best but dull and hoary,
    Mere glimmerings and decays.

O holy Hope, and high Humility,
    High as the heavens above!
These are your walks, and you have showed them me,
    To kindle my cold love.

Dear, beauteous Death, the jewel of the just,
    Shining nowhere but in the dark,
What mysteries do lie beyond thy dust,
    Could man outlook that mark!

He that hath found some fledg'd bird's nest may know,
    At first sight, if the bird be flown;
But what fair field or grove he sings in now,
    That is to him unknown.

And yet as angels, in some brighter dreams,
    Call to the soul when man doth sleep,
So some strange thoughts transcend our wonted themes,
    And into glory peep.

If a star were confined into a tomb,
    Her captive flame must needs burn there;
But when the hand that locked her up gave room,
    She'd shine through all the sphere.

O Father of eternal life, and all
    Created glories under Thee!
Resume my spirit from this world of thrall
    Into true liberty.

Either disperse these mists, which blot and fill
    My perspective, still, as they pass;
Or else remove me hence unto that hill,
    Where I shall need no glass.

TO THE HOLY BIBLE.

O BOOK! life's guide! how shall we part?
And thou so long seized of my heart!
Take this last kiss; and let me weep
True thanks to thee before I sleep.

Thou wert the first put in my hand,
When yet I could not understand,
And daily didst my young eyes lead
To letters, till I learned to read.
But as rash youths, when once grown strong,
Fly from their nurses to the throng
Where they new consorts choose, and stick
To those till either hurt or sick;
So with that first light gained from thee
Ran I in chase of vanity,
Cried dross for gold, and never thought
My first cheap book had all I sought.
Long reigned this vogue; and thou, cast by,
With meek dumb looks didst woo mine eye,

And oft, left open, would convey
A sudden and most searching ray
Into my soul, with whose quick touch,
Repining, still I struggled much.
By this mild art of love at length
Thou overcam'st my sinful strength,
And having brought me home, didst there
Show me that pearl I sought elsewhere.
Gladness, and peace, and hope, and love,
The secret favours of the Dove;
Her quickening kindness, smiles, and kisses,
Exalted pleasures, crowning blisses,
Fruition, union, glory, life,
Thou didst lead to; and still all strife.
Living, thou wert my soul's sure ease,
And dying, mak'st me go in peace:
Thy next effects no tongue can tell;
Farewell, O Book of God! Farewell!

"I HAVE LEARNED IN WHATSOEVER STATE I AM THEREWITH
TO BE CONTENT."

To such great mercies what shall I prefer?
Or who from loving God shall me deter?
Burn me alive with curious skilful pain,
Cut up and search each warm and breathing vein;
When all is done death brings a quick release,
And the poor mangled body sleeps in peace.
Hale me to prisons, shut me up in brass:
My still free soul from thence to God shall pass.

Banish or bind me; I can be nowhere
A stranger or alone; my God is there.
I fear not famine. How can he be said
To starve who feeds upon the living bread?
And yet this courage springs not from my store;
Christ gave it me, who can give much, much more.
I of myself can nothing dare or do;
He bids me fight; and makes me conquer too.
If like great Abraham I should have command
To leave my father's house and native land,
I would with joy to unknown regions run,
Bearing the banner of his blessed Son.
On worldly goods I will have no design;
But use my own, as if mine were not mine.
Wealth I'll not wonder at, nor greatness seek,
But choose, though laughed at, to be poor and meek.
In love and wealth, I'll keep the same staid mind;
Grief shall not break me, nor joys make me blind.

'Life of Paulinus.'

JOHN MILTON.

BORN A.D. 1608; DIED A.D. 1674.

THIS greatest of English Poets was a native of the city of London, having been born in Bread Street, Cheapside, December 9th, 1608, where his father was in business as a scrivener. John Milton was educated at St. Paul's School, whence he proceeded to Christ's College, Cambridge. After residing at the University for seven years he returned to his father's house, at Horton, in Buckinghamshire. It was at this period of his life that many of his noblest works were composed. In 1638, he left England and travelled on the Continent, till he was recalled by the news of the breaking out of the Civil War. On his return he occupied himself in teaching, and soon distinguished himself by the support he gave by his writings to the cause of the Parliament. During the Protectorate, he was Latin secretary to Oliver Cromwell. After the Restoration, he was treated with lenity, though his celebrated works written in defence of the Parliament, *Iconoclastes* and *Defensio Populi Anglicani*, were burned by the common hangman. He lived in obscurity in Jewin Street, from whence he moved to Bunhill Fields. For some years before his death he was perfectly blind, and dictated his later poems, *Paradise Lost*, *Paradise Regained*, and *Samson Agonistes*, to amanuenses. He died on November 8th, 1674, and was buried in the Church of St. Giles, Cripplegate.

It may perhaps seem strange that the extracts given from the works of this wonderful man are so few; but though by far the largest part of his poems are connected with sacred subjects, their allegorical, descriptive, and dramatic character, renders them hardly so suitable to the object of the present work, as those of men of humbler genius and accomplishments, but whose writings are more strictly personal and devotional, and are, at the same time, less generally known.

SONNET ON THE MASSACRE OF THE WALDENSES.

AVENGE, O Lord, Thy slaughter'd saints, whose bones
Lie scatter'd on the Alpine mountains cold;
E'en them who kept Thy truth so pure of old,
When all our fathers worshipp'd stocks and stones,
Forget not: in Thy book record their groans

Who were Thy sheep, and in their ancient fold
Slain by the bloody Piemontese, that roll'd
Mother with infant down the rocks. The moans
The vales redoubled to the hills, and they
To heaven. Their martyr'd blood and ashes sow
O'er all the Italian fields, where still doth sway
The triple tyrant; that from these may grow
A hundredfold, who, having learn'd Thy way,
Early may fly the Babylonian woe.

ON HIS BLINDNESS.

When I consider how my light is spent
Ere half my days, in this dark world and wide,
And that one talent, which is death to hide,
Lodged with me useless, though my soul more bent
To serve therewith my Maker, and present
My true account, lest He, returning, chide;—
"Doth God exact day-labour, light denied?"
I fondly ask : but Patience, to prevent
That murmur, soon replies, "God doth not need
Either man's work, or his own gifts; who best
Bear his mild yoke, they serve Him best : his state
Is kingly; thousands at his bidding speed,
And post o'er land and ocean without rest;
They also serve who only stand and wait."

PRAISE IN HEAVEN.

No sooner had the Almighty ceased, but all
The multitude of angels, with a shout
Loud as from numbers without number, sweet
As from blest voices, utt'ring joy, heav'n rang

MILTON AND HIS DAUGHTERS.

With jubilee, and loud hosannas fill'd
Th' eternal regions: lowly reverent
Towards either throne they bow, and to the ground,
With solemn adoration, down they cast
Their crowns inwove with amarant and gold;
Immortal amarant, a flower which once
In Paradise, fast by the tree of life,
Began to bloom; but soon for man's offence
To heaven removed, where first it grew, there grows
And flowers aloft, shading the fount of life,
And where the river of bliss through midst of heaven
Rolls o'er Elysian flowers her amber stream:
With these, that never fade, the spirits elect
Bind their resplendent locks inwreath'd with beams.
Now, in loose garlands thick thrown off, the bright
Pavement, that like a sea of jasper shone,
Impurpled with celestial roses, smiled;
Then, crown'd again, their golden harps they took,
Harps ever tuned, that glittering by their side
Like quivers hung, and with preamble sweet
Of charming symphony they introduce
Their sacred song, and waken raptures high;
No voice exempt, no voice but well could join
Melodious part, such concord is in heaven.
'Paradise Lost,' Book III.

THE MORNING HYMN OF ADAM AND EVE.

"THESE are Thy glorious works,—Parent of good,
Almighty! Thine this universal frame,
Thus wondrous fair; Thyself how wondrous then!
Unspeakable, who sitt'st above these heavens

To us invisible, or dimly seen
In these thy lowest works; yet these declare
Thy goodness beyond thought, and power divine.
Speak, ye who best can tell, ye sons of light,
Angels; for ye behold Him, and with songs
And choral symphonies, day without night,
Circle His throne rejoicing; ye in heaven,
On earth join all ye creatures to extol
Him first, Him last, Him midst, and without end.
Fairest of stars, last in the train of night,
If better Thou belong not to the dawn,
Sure pledge of day, that crown'st the smiling morn
With Thy bright circlet, praise Him in thy sphere,
While day arises, that sweet hour of prime.
Thou Sun, of this great world both eye and soul,
Acknowledge Him thy greater; sound His praise
In thy eternal course, both when thou climb'st,
And when high noon hast gain'd, and when thou fall'st.
Moon, that now meet'st the orient Sun, now fly'st,
With the fix'd stars, fix'd in their orb that flies;
And ye five other wandering fires, that move
In mystic dance not without song, resound
His praise, who out of darkness call'd up light.
Air, and ye elements, the eldest birth
Of Nature's womb, that in quaternion run
Perpetual circle, multiform, and mix
And nourish all things; let your ceaseless change
Vary to our great Maker still new praise.
Ye mists and exhalations, that now rise
From hill or steaming lake, dusky, or gray,
Till the Sun paint your fleecy skirts with gold,
In honour to the World's great Author rise;
Whether to deck with clouds the uncoloured sky,

Or wet the thirsty earth with falling showers,
Rising or falling still advance His praise.
His praise, ye winds, that from four quarters blow,
Breathe soft or loud; and wave your tops, ye pines,
With every plant, in sign of worship wave.
Fountains, and ye that warble, as ye flow,
Melodious murmurs, warbling tune His praise.
Join voices, all ye living souls: ye birds,
That singing up to heaven-gate ascend,
Bear on your wings and in your notes His praise.
Ye that in waters glide, and ye that walk
The earth, and stately tread, or lowly creep;
Witness if I be silent, morn or even,
To hill or valley, fountain, or fresh shade,
Made vocal by my song, and taught His praise.
Hail, universal Lord, be bounteous still
To give us only good; and if the night
Have gather'd aught of evil or conceal'd,
Disperse it, as now light dispels the dark!"

       'Paradise Lost,' Book V.

THE FIRST SABBATH.

AND now on earth the seventh
Evening arose in Eden, for the sun
Was set, and twilight from the east came on,
Forerunning night; when at the holy mount
Of Heaven's high seated top, the imperial throne
Of Godhead, fix'd for ever firm and sure,

The Filial Power arrived, and sat Him down
With His great Father; for he also went
Invisible, yet stay'd (such privilege
Hath Omnipresence), and the work ordained,
Author and end of all things; and, from work
Now resting, blessed and hallowed the seventh day,
As resting on that day from all His work;
But not in silence holy kept : the harp
Had work and rested not; the solemn pipe
And dulcimer, all organs of sweet stop,
All sounds on fret by string or golden wire,
Temper'd soft tunings, intermix'd with voice,
Choral or unison; of incense, clouds
Fuming from golden censers hid the mount.
Creation and the six days' acts they sung :
Great are Thy works, Jehovah! infinite
Thy power! what tongue can measure Thee, or tongue
Relate Thee! greater now in Thy return
Than from the giant angels: Thee that day
Thy thunders magnified; but to create
Is greater than created to destroy.
Who can impair Thee, mighty King, or bound
Thy empire? Easily the proud attempt
Of spirits apostate, and their counsels vain,
Thou hast repelled; while impiously they thought
Thee to diminish, and from Thee withdraw
The number of Thy worshippers. Who seeks
To lessen Thee, against his purpose serves
To manifest the more Thy might; his evil
Thou usest, and from thence creat'st more good.
Witness this new made world, another heaven!
From heaven-gate not far, founded in view
On the clear hyaline, the glassy sea,

Of amplitude almost immense, with stars
Numerous, and every star perhaps a world
Of destined habitation ; but Thou know'st
Their seasons ; among these the seat of Men,
Earth, with her nether ocean circumfused,
Their pleasant dwelling-place. Thrice happy Men,
And sons of Men, whom God hath thus advanced !
Created in His image, there to dwell
And worship Him ; and in reward to rule·
Over his works, on earth, in sea, or air,
And multiply a race of worshippers
Holy and just : thrice happy, if they know
Their happiness, and persevere upright.
   So sung they, and the empyréan rung
With hallelujahs : thus was Sabbath kept.
' Paradise Lost,' Book VII.

ODE—AT A SOLEMN MUSIC.

BLEST pairs of sirens, pledges of heaven's joy,
Sphere-born, harmonious sisters, Voice and Verse,
Wed your Divine sounds, and mixed power employ,
Dead things with inbreathed sense able to pierce ;
And to our high-raised phantasy present
That undisturbèd song of pure consent,
Aye sung before the sapphire-coloured throne,
To Him that sits thereon,
With saintly shout and solemn jubilee ;
Where the bright seraphim in burning row,

Their loud up-lifted angel-trumpets blow;
And the cherubic host, in thousand quires,
Touch their immortal harps of golden wires,
With those just spirits that wear victorious palms,
Hymns devout and holy psalms
Singing everlastingly :
That we on earth, with undiscording voice,
May rightly answer that melodious noise ;
As once we did, till disproportioned sin
Jarr'd against nature's chime, and with harsh din
Broke the fair music that all creatures made
To their great Lord, whose love their motion sway'd
In perfect diapason, whilst they stood
In first obedience and their state of good.
Oh may we soon again renew that song,
And keep in tune with heaven, till God ere long
To his celestial concert us unite,
To live with Him, and sing in endless morn of light!

SAMSON, BEWAILING HIS BLINDNESS AND CAPTIVITY.

A LITTLE onward lend thy guiding hand
To these dark steps, a little further on ;
For yonder bank hath choice of sun or shade :
There I am wont to sit, when any chance
Relieves me from my task of servile toil,
Daily in the common prison else enjoin'd me,
Where I, a prisoner chain'd, scarce freely draw
The air imprison'd also, close and damp,

Unwholesome draught : but here I feel amends,
The breath of heaven fresh blowing, pure and sweet,
With day-spring born ; here leave me to respire.—
This day a solemn feast the people hold
To Dagon their sea-idol, and forbid
Laborious works; unwillingly this rest
Their superstition yields me ; hence with leave
Retiring from the popular noise, I seek
This unfrequented place to find some ease,
Ease to the body some, none to the mind
From restless thoughts, that, like a deadly swarm
Of hornets arm'd, no sooner found alone,
But rush upon me thronging, and present
Times past, what once I was, and what am now.
Oh, wherefore was my birth from heaven foretold
Twice by an angel, who at last in sight
Of both my parents all in flames ascended
From off the altar, where an offering burn'd,
As in a fiery column, charioting
His godlike presence, and from some great act
Or benefit reveal'd to Abraham's race ?
Why was my breeding order'd and prescribed
As of a person separate to God,
Design'd for great exploits, if I must die
Betray'd, captived, and both my eyes put out,
Made of my enemies the scorn and gaze ?

* * * *

Oh, dark, dark, dark, amid the blaze of noon,
Irrecoverably dark, total eclipse
Without all hope of day !
O first created Beam, and thou great Word,
' Let there be light ! and light was over all ;'
Why am I thus bereaved thy prime decree ?

The sun to me is dark,
And silent as the moon
When she deserts the night,
Hid in her vacant interlunar cave.
Since light so necessary is to life,
And almost life itself, if it be true
That light is in the soul,
She all in every part; why was the sight
To such a tender ball as the eye confined,
So obvious and so easy to be quench'd?
And not, as feeling, through all parts diffused,
That she might look at will through every pore?
Then had I not been thus exiled from light,
As in the land of darkness yet in light,
To live a life half dead, a living death,
And buried: but, oh yet more miserable!
Myself my sepulchre, a moving grave;
Buried, yet not exempt
By privilege of death and burial,
From worst of other evils, pains, and wrongs;
But made hereby obnoxious more
To all the miseries of life,
Life in captivity
Among inhuman foes.

'Samson Agonistes.'

SIR THOMAS BROWNE.

BORN A.D. 1605; DIED A.D. 1682.

SIR THOMAS BROWNE was born in London in 1605. He received a liberal education at Winchester and Oxford. After travelling on the continent for some time, he settled down in practice as a physician, first near Halifax, but soon afterwards at Norwich, where the rest of his life was spent. He was knighted in 1671, when Charles II. was visiting that city, and there he died peacefully in a good old age in 1682.

His writings enjoyed a wonderful popularity in his lifetime, and they have still a charm which is peculiarly their own, being the productions of one who, it has been said, was at once "an acute observer, a fanciful speculator, a brilliant essayist, an amiable physician, a considerate, thoughtful paterfamilias." He was, too, a man of deep and earnest piety, though the forms in which his religion expressed itself were sometimes fanciful and eccentric. He who laid down the following rules for the guidance of his daily life was surely full of the fear of God and the love of man :—" To pray and magnify God in the night when I could not sleep : to know no street nor passage in this city which may not witness that I have not forgot my God and Saviour in it. Since the necessities of the sick, and unavoidable diversions of my profession, keep me often from church, yet to take all possible care that I might never miss sacraments on their appointed days. Upon sight of beautiful persons, to bless God in his creatures, to pray for the beauty of their souls, and to enrich them with inward graces to be answerable unto the outward. Upon sight of deformed persons, to send them inward graces and enrich their souls, and give them the beauty of the resurrection."

We can quite understand how he who wrote thus, should write also the following hymn, interesting for its own and its author's sake, and because it plainly contains the germ of Bishop Ken's evening hymn. It is from the *Religio Medici*, published in 1642.

EVENING HYMN.

THE night is come ; like to the day,
Depart not Thou, great God, away ;
Let not my sins, black as the night,
Eclipse the lustre of Thy light.

Keep still in my horizon, for to me
The sun makes not the day, but Thee.
Thou whose nature cannot sleep,
On my temples sentry keep;
Guard me 'gainst those watchful foes,
Whose eyes are open while mine close.
Let no dreams my head infest,
But such as Jacob's temples bless'd.
While I do rest, my soul advance,
Make my sleep a holy trance:
That I may, my rest being wrought,
Awake into some holy thought;
And with as active vigour run
My course as doth the nimble sun.
Sleep is a death;—oh make me try,
By sleeping, what it is to die!
And as gently lay my head
On my grave, as now my bed.
Howe'er I rest, great God, let me
Awake again at last with Thee.
And thus assured, behold, I lie
Securely, or to wake or die.
These are my drowsy days; in vain
I do now sleep to wake again:
Oh, come that hour when I shall never
Sleep again, but wake for ever!

WALLER'S TOMB AT BEACONSFIELD.

EDMUND WALLER.

BORN A.D. 1605; DIED A.D. 1687.

WALLER was descended from an old and wealthy Kentish family; he was the son of Robert Waller of Amersham in Buckinghamshire. His mother was the sister of John Hampden, and cousin to Oliver Cromwell. He entered the House of Commons at a very early age, and began his public life on the side of the Parliament. But he seems to have been a royalist at heart; and in 1643, he was concerned in a plot in behalf of the king, for which he was banished and fined £10,000. He remained in exile for ten years, when he obtained permission to return, and resided on his estate at Beaconsfield. He was on friendly terms with Cromwell, and on his death wrote his panegyric. After the Restoration he was a favourite at the courts of Charles II. and James II. He died at his house at Beaconsfield, at the advanced age of eighty-two. His *Divine Poems*, from which the following extracts are taken, were composed shortly before his death. He says in them,—

> Wrestling with death, these lines I did indite;
> No other theme could give my soul delight.
> Oh that my youth had thus employed my pen!
> Or that I now could write as well as then!

But 'tis of grace; if sickness, age and pain,
Are felt as throes when we are born again,
Timely they come to wean us from this earth,
As pangs that wait upon a second birth.

THE LOVE OF GOD.

I.—IN CREATION.

THAT early love of creatures yet unmade,
To frame the world th' Almighty did persuade;
For love it was that, first, created light,
Moved on the waters, chased away the night
From the rude chaos, and bestowed new grace
On things disposed of to their proper place;
Some to rest here, and some to shine above;
Earth, sea, and heaven, were all the effects of love.
And love would be returned; but there was none
That to themselves or others yet were known;
The world a palace was without a guest,
Till one appears that must excel the rest;
One like the Author, whose capacious mind
Might, by the glorious work, the Maker find;
Might measure heaven, and give each star a name;
With art and courage the rough ocean tame;
Over the globe with swelling sails might go,
And that 'tis round by his experience know;
Make strongest beasts obedient to his will,
And serve his use, the fertile earth to till.
When, by His Word, God had accomplished all,
Man to create, He did a council call;
Employed His hand, to give the dust He took
A graceful figure, and majestic look;

With His own breath conveyed into his breast
Life, and a soul fit to command the rest,
Worthy alone to celebrate His name,
For such a gift, and tell from whence it came
Birds sing His praises in a wilder note,
But not with lasting numbers, and with thought,
Man's great prerogative! but above all,
His grace abounds in His new favourite's fall.
  If He create, it is a world He makes;
If He be angry, the creation shakes;
From His just wrath our guilty parents fled;
He cursed the earth, but bruised the serpent's head.
Amidst the storm His bounty did exceed
In the rich promise of the Virgin's seed;
Though Justice death, as satisfaction, craves,
Love finds a way to pluck us from our graves.

II.—IN REDEMPTION.

NOT willing terror should His image move,
He gives a pattern of eternal love;
His Son descends, to treat a peace with those
Which were, and must have ever been, his foes.
Poor He became, and left His glorious seat,
To make us humble, and to make us great;
His business here was happiness to give
To those whose malice could not let Him live.
Legions of angels, which He might have used,
For us resolved to perish, He refused;
While they stood ready to prevent His loss,
Love took Him up and nailed Him to the cross.

Immortal Love! which in His bowels reigned,
That we might be by such high love constrained
To make return of love; upon this pole
Our duty does and our religion roll.
To love is to believe, to hope, to know;
'Tis an essay, a taste of heaven below.
He to proud potentates would not be known;
Of those that loved Him He was hid from none.
Till love appear, we live in anxious doubt;
But smoke will vanish when that flame breaks out.
This is the fire that would consume our dross,
Refine and make us richer by the loss.
Could we forbear dispute and practise love,
We should agree as angels do above.
Where Love presides, not vice alone does find
No entrance there, but virtues stay behind.
Both Faith and Hope, and all the meaner train
Of moral virtues, at the door remain;
Love only enters as a native there,
For born in heaven, it does but sojourn here.
He that alone could wise and mighty be,
Commands that others love as well as He.
Love as He loved! how can we soar so high?
He can add wings when He commands to fly.
Nor should we be with this command dismayed,
He that examples gives will give His aid;
For He took flesh, that, where His precepts fail,
His practice as a pattern may prevail;
His love at once, and dread, instruct our thought—
As man He suffered, and as God He taught.
Will for the deed He takes; we may with ease
Obedient be, for if we love we please;
Weak though we are, to love is no hard task,

And love for love is all that heaven does ask :
Love that would all men just and temperate make,
Kind to themselves and others, for His sake.
'Tis with our minds as with a fertile ground,
Wanting this love, they must with weeds abound ;
Unruly passions, whose effects are worse
Than thorns and thistles springing from the curse.

      ' Divine Love,' Cantos II. III.

CONCLUSION OF THE "DIVINE POEMS."

THE seas are quiet when the winds are o'er,
So calm are we when passions are no more ;
For then we know how vain it was to boast
Of fleeting things, so certain to be lost.
Clouds of affection from our younger eyes
Conceal that emptiness which age descries.

The soul's dark cottage, battered and decayed,
Lets in new light through chinks that time has made.
Stronger by weakness, wiser men become,
As they draw near to their eternal home :
Leaving the old, both worlds at once they view
That stand upon the threshold of the new.

JOHN DRYDEN.

BORN A.D. 1631; DIED A.D. 1700.

DRYDEN has few claims to a place in a collection of sacred poetry. Living in an age of the utmost licence and impurity, his writings are stained with the vices of the times. He was, however, resolutely opposed to the infidelity then so rife, and in his *Religio Laici* he has asserted, in vigorous verse, the claims of revelation and the duty of faith. He was born of a good family, at Aldwinkle, in Northamptonshire, and received his education at Westminster and Trinity College, Cambridge. On the death of his father, in 1654, he came to London, and was received into the family of his relative, Sir Gilbert Pickering, who was a member of Cromwell's council. Though he had written a panegyric on the death of the Protector, he yet greeted the return of Charles by a poem entitled *Astræa Redux*. This, with many other laudatory pieces, gained for him the royal favour, and, in 1668, he was appointed Poet Laureate and Historiographer to the King. He retained these offices till the abdication of James, when he lost all his emoluments and fell into poverty. During the last ten years of his life, he was reduced to the necessity of writing for bread. On his death, in the year 1700, he was buried in Westminster Abbey, between Chaucer and Cowley.

THE HOLY SCRIPTURES.

WHENCE but from heaven could men, unskilled in Arts,
In several ages born, in several parts,
Weave such agreeable truths? or how or why
Should all conspire to cheat us with a lie?
Unasked their pains, ungrateful their advice,
Starving their gain, and martyrdom their price.
　If on the book itself we cast our view,
Concurrent heathens prove the story true;
The doctrine, miracles, which must convince,
For Heaven in them appeals to human sense;

And though they prove not, they confirm the cause,
When what is taught agrees with nature's laws.
　Then for the style; majestic and divine,
It speaks no less than God in every line;
Commanding words, whose force is still the same,
As the first fiat that produced our frame.
　All faiths beside, or did by arms ascend,
Or sense indulged has made mankind their friend;
This only doctrine does our lusts oppose;
Unfed by nature's soil, on which it grows;
Cross to our interests, curbing sense and sin,
Oppressed without, and undermined within,
It thrives through pain, its own tormentors tires,
And with a stubborn patience still aspires.
To what can reason such effects assign,
Transcending nature, but to laws Divine,
Which in that sacred volume are contained,
Sufficient, clear, and for that use ordained.

x

RICHARD BAXTER.

BORN A.D. 1615; DIED A.D. 1691.

THIS celebrated man, so learned and holy, and who endured so much in what he felt to be the cause of Christ, was born at the village of Rowton in Shropshire. Having received a good education, he was ordained, in 1638, by Dr. Thornborough, Bishop of Winchester, and soon afterwards settled at Kidderminster, where, for sixteen years, he zealously discharged the duties of a parochial minister. His sympathies were on the side of the Parliament, and he acted, after the battle of Naseby, as chaplain to Colonel Whalley's regiment. On the Restoration, in which he heartily concurred, he received some marks of royal favour, being made royal chaplain, and having the Bishopric of Hereford offered him. But he was not thus drawn away from the party whose cause he had espoused. He acted as one of the Commissioners who represented the Nonconformists at the Savoy Conference. During the reigns of Charles II. and James II. he was subject to frequent interruptions and persecutions in the work of the ministry, which however he continued to exercise up to the close of his long life. In 1685, he was tried for sedition on account of certain passages in his paraphrase of the New Testament. The treatment he met with from the infamous Jeffreys is well known. He was fined and imprisoned, but was released in the following year, and died in 1691. He was a most voluminous writer. His practical works alone consist of 112 separate publications, which form four large folio volumes. Amongst these are some "Poetical Fragments," from which the following pieces are selected.

THE COVENANT AND CONFIDENCE OF FAITH.

My whole, though broken heart, O Lord,
From henceforth shall be Thine;
And here I do my vow record:
This hand, these words are mine.
All that I have, without reserve,
I offer here to Thee:
Thy will and honour, all, shall serve,
That Thou bestow'dst on me.

All that exceptions save I lose ;
 All that I lose I save :
The treasure of Thy love I choose ;
 And Thou art all I crave.
My God, Thou hast my heart and hand ;
 I all to Thee resign :
I'll ever to this covenant stand,
 Though flesh hereat repine.

I know that Thou wast willing first,
 And then mad'st me consent :
Having thus loved me at the worst,
 Thou wilt not now repent.
Now I have quit all self-pretence,
 Take charge of what's Thine own ;
My life, my health, and my defence,
 Now lie on Thee alone.

Now it belongs not to my care,
 Whether I die or live ;
To love and serve Thee is my share :
 And this Thy grace must give.
If life be long, I will be glad,
 That I may long obey :
If short—yet why should I be sad,
 That shall have the same pay.

If death shall bruise this springing seed,
 Before it come to fruit,
The will with Thee goes for the deed—
 Thy life was in the root.

Long life is a long grief and toil,
    And multiplieth faults;
In long wars he may have the foil
    That 'scaped in short assaults.

Would I long bear my heavy load,
    And keep my sorrows long?
Would I long sin against my God,
    And His dear mercy wrong?
How much is sinful flesh my foe,
    That doth my soul pervert;
To linger here in sin and woe,
    And steal from God my heart.

Christ leads me through no darker rooms
    Than He went through before;
He that into God's kingdom comes
    Must enter by this door.
Come, Lord, when grace hath made me meet
    Thy blessed face to see:
For if Thy work on earth be sweet,
    What will Thy glory be?

Then I shall end my sad complaints,
    And weary, sinful days,
And join with the triumphant saints
    That sing Jehovah's praise.
My knowledge of that life is small;
    The eye of faith is dim:
But it's enough that Christ knows all,
    And I shall be with Him.

A PSALM OF PRAISE.

THE FIRST PART.

Ye holy angels bright,
  Which stand before God's throne,
And dwell in glorious light,
  Praise ye the Lord each one!
    You there so nigh,
    Fitter than we
    Dark sinners be
    For things so high.

You blessed souls at rest,
  Who see your Saviour's face,
Whose glory, e'en the least,
  Is far above our grace;
    God's praises sound
    As, in His sight,
    With sweet delight,
    You do abound.

All nations of the earth,
  Extol the world's great King!
With melody and mirth
  His glorious praises sing;
    For He still reigns,
    And will bring low
    The proudest foe
    That Him disdains.

Sing forth Jehovah's praise,
  Ye saints that on Him call!
Magnify Him always,
  His holy churches all!
    In Him rejoice,
    And there proclaim
    His holy name
    With sounding voice.

My soul, bear thou thy part:
  Triumph in God above!
With a well-tunèd heart,
  Sing thou the songs of love!
    Thou art His own,
    Whose precious blood,
    Shed for thy good,
    His love made known.

He did in love begin,
  Renewing thee by grace,
Forgiving all thy sin,
  Show'd thee His pleasèd face;
    He did thee heal
    By his own merit:
    And by his spirit
    He did thee seal.

In saddest thoughts and grief,
  In sickness, fears, and pain,
I cried for His relief,
  And did not cry in vain.

He heard with speed,
And still I found
Mercy abound
In time of need.

Let not His praises grow
On prosperous heights alone,
But in the vales below
Let His great love be known.
Let no distress
Curb and control
My wingèd soul,
And praise suppress.

DARTMOUTH

JOHN FLAVEL.

BORN A.D. 1627; DIED A.D. 1691.

This eminent minister of the gospel is best known by his prose writings, in which the truth is so powerfully, plainly, and attractively set forth. His work entitled *Husbandry Spiritualized*, which he wrote for the benefit of the rural population among whom he laboured, contains many short poems, from which the following extracts are taken. He was the son of a clergyman at Bromsgrove, in Worcestershire, and was himself Minister of Dartmouth, in Devonshire, from which living he was ejected on the passing of the Act of Uniformity. He continued, however, to exercise his ministry in the neighbourhood, as far as was possible under the intolerant laws which were in force, during the greater part of his life. He died at Exeter, June 26, 1691. His body was conveyed to Dartmouth, and buried in the church, amid crowds of mourners, who flocked from all the country near to testify their affectionate remembrance of him.

GOD'S HUSBANDRY.

THOU art the Husbandman, and I
A worthless plot of husbandry,
Whom special love did, ne'ertheless,
Divide from nature's wilderness.
  Then did the sunshine of Thy face,
And sweet illapses of Thy grace,
Like April showers and warming gleams,
Distil their dews, reflect their beams.
My dead affections then were green,
And hopeful buds on them were seen;
These into duties soon were turn'd,
In which my heart within me burn'd.
  O halcyon-days! thrice happy state!
Each place was Bethel, heaven's gate.
What sweet discourse, what heavenly talk,
While with Thee I did daily walk!
Mine eyes o'erflow, my heart doth sink,
As oft as on those days I think.
For strangeness now is come between
My God and me, as may be seen
By what is now, and what was then:
'Tis just as if I were two men!
My fragrant branches blasted be,
No fruits like those that I can see;
Some canker-worm lies at my root,
Which fades my leaves, destroys my fruit;
My soul is banish'd from Thy sight,
For this it mourneth day and night.
  Yet why dost thou desponding lie?
With Jonah, cast a backward eye.

That God who made me spring at first,
When I was barren and accurs'd,
Can much more easily restore
My state to what it was before :
A word, a smile on my poor soul
Would make it perfect, sound, and whole.

THE GROWTH OF GRACE.

'Tis justly wondered that an ear of corn
Should come at last in safety to the barn.
It runs through many hazards, threatening harms,
Betwixt the sower's hands, and reaper's arms.

    *   *   *   *

Thus saving grace, that precious seed of joy,
Which hell and nature plot how to destroy,
Escapes ten thousand dangers first and last.
Oh who can say, Now all the danger's past?
'Tis like a crazy bark tossed in a storm,
Or like a taper which is strangely borne,
Without a lantern, in a blustering night;
Or like to glimmering sparks, whose dying light
Is still preserved. The roaring waves swell high,
Like moving mountains in the darkened sky;
On their proud backs, the little bark is even
Mounted unto the battlements of heaven,
From thence, dismounted, to the deeps doth slide,
Receiving water upon every side;
Yet He whose voice the proudest waves obey,
Brings it at last into the quiet quay.

"A FIELD WHICH THE LORD HATH BLESSED."

As when the sun draws near us in the spring,
All creatures do rejoice;—birds chirp and sing;
The face of nature smiles; the fields adorn
Themselves with rich embroideries; the corn
Revives and shooteth up; the warm, sweet rain
Makes trees and herbs sprout forth, and spring amain.
Walk but the fields in such a fragrant morn,
How do the birds your ears with music charm!
The flowers their flaming beauties do present
Unto your captiv'd eyes; and for their scent,
The sweet Arabian gums cannot compare,
Which thus perfume the circumambient air.
 So, when the gospel sheds its cheering beams
On gracious souls, like those sweet warming gleams,
Which God ordains in nature, to draw forth
The virtue seminal that's in the earth,
It warms their hearts, their languid graces cheers,
And on such souls a spring-like face appears;
The gracious showers these spiritual clouds do yield,
Enriching them with sweetness, like a field
Which God hath bless'd.—Oh! 'tis exceeding sweet,
When humble hearts and heavenly truths do meet.
How should the hearts of saints within them spring,
When they behold the messengers, that bring
These gladsome tidings;—yea, their very feet
Are beautiful, because their words are sweet.
Thrice happy land! which, in this pleasant spring,
Can hear these turtles in her hedges sing.

THE GREEN HOUSE, ELSTOW.

JOHN BUNYAN.

BORN A.D. 1628; DIED A.D. 1688.

It is not needful to write the memoir of a life so well known as that of the author of the *Pilgrim's Progress*. We need only remind the reader that John Bunyan was the son of a tinker at Elstow, in Bedfordshire; that he became minister of the Baptist congregation at Bedford; that after the Restoration he was tried on the charge of holding unlawful assemblies and conventicles; that he was imprisoned for twelve years; that during his incarceration he wrote his immortal allegory; that he died in London, 1688, and was interred in the burial ground at Bunhill Fields.

STANZAS EXTRACTED FROM HIS MEDITATIONS ON "HEAVEN."

ALL mysteries shall here be seen,
And every knot untied;
Electing love, that hid hath been,
Shall shine on every side.

JOHN BUNYAN.

That head that once was crown'd with thorns,
    Shall now with glory shine ;
That heart that broken was with scorns,
    Shall flow with life divine.

What gladness shall possess our heart
    When we shall see these things ;
What light and life in every part
    Will rise like lasting springs.

O blessèd face and holy grace ;
    When shall we see this day ?
Lord, fetch us to this goodly place,
    We humbly do Thee pray.

Angels also we shall behold,
    When we on high ascend,
Each shining like to men of gold :
    And on the Lord attend.

These goodly creatures, full of grace,
    Shall stand about the throne,
Each one with lightning in his face,
    And shall to us be known.

These will us in their arms embrace,
    And welcome us to rest,
And joy to see us clad with grace,
    And of the heavens possess'd.

Our friends that livèd godly here,
    Shall there be found again ;
The wife, the child, and father dear,
    With others of our train.

Each one, down to the foot in white,
Fill'd to the brim with grace,
Walking among the saints in light,
With glad and joyful face.

This is the place, this is the state,
Of all that fear the Lord;
Which men nor angels may relate
With tongue, or pen, or word.

No night is here, for to eclipse
Its spangling rays so bright,
Nor doubt, nor fear to shut the lips
Of those within this light.

The strings of music here are tun'd
For heavenly harmony,
And every spirit here perfum'd
With perfect sanctity.

THE SWALLOW.

This pretty bird, oh, how she flies and sings!
But could she do so if she had not wings?
Her wings bespeak my faith, her songs my peace;
When I believe and sing, my doubtings cease.

JOHN BUNYAN.

THE FLINT IN THE WATER.

This flint, time out of mind has there abode,
Where crystal streams make their continual road,
Yet it abides a flint, as much as 'twere
Before it touched the water, or came there.
  Its hardness is not in the least abated,
'Tis not at all by water penetrated.
Though water hath a softening virtue in't,
It can't dissolve the stone, for 'tis a flint.
  Yea, though in water it doth still remain,
Its fiery nature still it doth retain;
If you oppose it with its opposite,
Then in your very face its fire 'twill spit.

  This flint an emblem is of those that lie
Under the word, like stones, until they die.
Its crystal streams have not their natures changed,
They are not from their lusts by grace estranged.

PRISON MEDITATIONS.

I am indeed in prison now
  In body, but my mind
Is free to study Christ, and how
  Unto me He is kind.

For though men keep my outward man
    Within their locks and bars,
Yet, by the faith of Christ, I can
    Mount higher than the stars.

Their fetters cannot spirits tame,
    Nor tie up God from me :
My faith and hope they cannot lame,
    Above them I shall be.

To them that here for evil lie,
    The place is comfortless ;
But not to me, because that I
    Lie here for righteousness.

Though men do say, we do disgrace
    Ourselves by lying here
Among the rogues, yet Christ our face
    From all such filth will clear.

We know there's neither flout nor frown
    That we now for Him bear,
But will add to our heavenly crown
    When He comes in the air ;

When He our righteousness forth brings,
    Bright shining as the day,
And wipeth off those slanderous things
    That scorners on us lay.

We sell our earthly happiness
    For heavenly house and home ;
We leave this world because 'tis less,
    And worse than that to come.

We change our drossy dust for gold,
  From death to life we fly:
We let go shadows, and take hold
  Of immortality.

We trade for that which lasting is,
  And nothing for it give,
But that which is already His
  By whom we breathe and live.

Oh, let us count those things the best
  That best will prove at last;
And count such men the only blest
  That do such things hold fast.

JEREMY TAYLOR, D.D.

BORN A.D. 1613; DIED A.D. 1667.

THIS celebrated man was the son of a barber at Cambridge. In 1626, he was admitted as a sizar, or poor scholar, at Caius College. He received ordination before he had attained the age of twenty-one, and shortly afterwards came up to London, where he attracted the notice of Archbishop Laud, by whom he was nominated to a fellowship at All Souls' College, Oxford. In 1638, we find him a royal chaplain. In the same year he was presented by Bishop Juxon, to the Rectory of Uppingham, where he zealously discharged his duties as a parochial clergyman. When the Civil war broke out, he was summoned to attend the king as his chaplain, and up to the time of Charles's flight to Scotland he continued with him, either at the headquarters of the army, or at Oxford, when the court was there. In 1645 or 1646, Taylor retired into Wales, where he supported himself by keeping a school. He subsequently found a safe shelter, and the support and consolation of true friendship, in the house of Lord Carbery, at Golden Grove, in Caermarthenshire. He officiated in the family as domestic chaplain, and from this retirement many of his most celebrated works were sent forth. In 1654, a Royalist insurrection was attempted. From his known attachment to that cause suspicion fell on him, and he was imprisoned in Chepstow Castle, but was, before long, set at liberty. In 1657, having suffered heavy domestic affliction in the loss of two of his children from small pox, he left Wales and came up to London, where, for a short time, he officiated privately to a congregation of Royalists. Soon, however, on the invitation of Lord Conway, he retired to that nobleman's seat, near Portmore, in the north of Ireland, and once more he found peaceful leisure for the exercise of his wonderful powers as a theological writer. At the Restoration he came again to London, and his name is affixed to the declaration of the Royalists published just before the return of the king, on April 24, 1660. Shortly afterwards, he was appointed Bishop of Down and Connor, and died at Lisburn, August 13, 1667, having continued to the last his unwearied literary labours.

He is better known for the wonderful richness and the glowing eloquence of his prose than for his poetry. In fact, there is so much poetry in his prose, that disappointment is sometimes felt in reading his verses; yet they are full of noble thoughts, though not free from the faults of style peculiar to his age. The following extracts are from the Festival Hymns which he appended to *The Golden Grove*, a manual of Christian faith and practice, published towards the close of his residence in Wales.

A PRAYER FOR CHARITY.

FULL of mercy, full of love,
Look upon us from above;
Thou, who taught'st the blind man's night
To entertain a double light,
Thine and the day's (and that Thine too);
The lame away his crutches threw;
The parchèd crust of leprosy
Return'd unto its infancy:
The dumb-amazèd was to hear
His own unchained tongue strike his ear:
Thy powerful mercy did e'en chase
The devil from his usurped place,
Where Thou thyself should'st dwell, not he.
Oh let Thy love our pattern be!
Let Thy mercy teach one brother
To forgive and love another;
That, copying Thy mercy here,
Thy goodness may hereafter rear
Our souls unto Thy glory, when
Our dust shall cease to be with men.

AN ADVENT HYMN.

LORD, come away;
Why dost Thou stay?
Thy road is ready; and Thy paths, made straight,
With longing expectation wait
The consecration of Thy beauteous feet.
Ride on triumphantly: behold, we lay
Our lusts and proud wills in Thy way.

Hosannah! welcome to our hearts; Lord, here
Thou hast a temple too, and full as dear
As that of Sion; and as full of sin;
Nothing but thieves and robbers dwell therein.
Enter, and chase them forth, and cleanse the floor;
Crucify them, that they may never more
 Profane that holy place,
 Where Thou hast chose to set Thy face.
And then if our stiff tongues shall be
Mute in the praises of Thy Deity,
 The stones out of the temple-wall
 Shall cry aloud and call
Hosannah! and Thy glorious footsteps greet.

HYMN FOR CHRISTMAS DAY.

MYSTERIOUS truth! that the selfsame should be
A Lamb, a Shepherd, and a Lion too!
   Yet such was He
 Whom first the shepherds knew,
 When they themselves became
 Sheep to the Shepherd Lamb.
Shepherd of men and angels,—Lamb of God,—
Lion of Judah,—by these titles keep
The wolf from thy endangered sheep.
 Bring all the world into Thy fold;
  Let Jews and Gentiles hither come
  In numbers great, that can't be told;
  And call Thy lambs, that wander, home.
 Glory be to God on high,
All glories to the glorious Deity!

THE ADORATION OF THE WISE MEN.

A COMET, dangling in the air,
Presaged the ruin both of death and sin ;
And told the wise men of a king,
The King of glory, and the Sun
Of righteousness, who then begun
To draw towards that blessèd hemisphere.
They, from the farthest east, this new
And unknown light pursue,
    Till they appear
In this blest infant King's propitious eye,
And pay their homage to His royalty.
Persia might then the rising sun adore ;
    It was idolatry no more.
    Great God, they gave to Thee
    Myrrh, frankincense, and gold :
    But Lord, with what shall we
Present ourselves before Thy majesty,
Whom Thou redeem'dst when we were sold :
    Vile dirt and clay?
    Yet it is soft, and may
    Impression take;
Accept it, Lord, and say, this Thou hadst rather;
Stamp it, and on this sordid metal make
    Thy holy image, and it shall outshine
    The beauty of the golden mine.

ANDREW MARVELL.

BORN A.D. 1620; DIED A.D. 1678.

ANDREW MARVELL was the son of a clergyman of the same name at Hull. Having completed his university education at Trinity College, Cambridge, he went abroad, and spent some years in foreign travel. On his return to England, in 1657, he became assistant to John Milton in his office of Latin Secretary. On the Restoration he was elected member of Parliament for Hull, and continued to be so till his death, nearly thirty years after. He was distinguished by the boldness of his satires and other writings in opposition to the supporters of arbitrary government, and by the inflexible integrity which enabled him to resist, though in needy circumstances, all the solicitations and bribes of his political opponents. We have but little of his poetry remaining, but enough has come down to us to show that he is entitled to a high place among our minor English Poets.

THE EMIGRANTS.

WHERE the remote Bermudas ride,
In ocean's bosom unespied,
From a small boat that rowed along,
The list'ning winds received this song.

"What should we do, but sing His praise
That led us through the watery maze,
Unto an isle so long unknown,
And yet far kinder than our own?

"Where He the huge sea-monsters racks,
That lift the deep upon their backs,
He lands us on a grassy stage,
Safe from the storms and prelates' rage.

"THUS SANG THEY, IN THE ENGLISH BOAT,
A HOLY AND A CHEERFUL NOTE."

"He gave us this eternal spring
Which here enamels everything,
And sends the fowls to us in care,
On daily visits through the air.

"He hangs in shades the orange bright,
Like golden lamps in a green night.
And does in the pomegranates close
Jewels more rich than Ormus shows.

"He makes the figs our mouths to meet,
And throws the melons at our feet;
But apples plants of such a price,
No tree could ever bear them twice.

"With cedars chosen by His hand
From Lebanon, He stores the land.
And makes the hollow seas that roar
Proclaim the ambergris on shore.

"He cast (of which we rather boast)
The Gospel pearl upon our coast.
And in these rocks for us did frame
A temple, where to sound His name.

Oh let our voice His praise exalt
Till it arrive at heaven's vault,
Which thence perhaps, rebounding may,
Echo beyond the Mexique bay."

Thus sang they, in the English boat,
A holy and a cheerful note,
And all the way, to guide their chime,
With falling oars they kept the time.

DIALOGUE BETWEEN THE RESOLVED SOUL AND CREATED PLEASURE.

COURAGE, my soul, now learn to wield
The weight of thine immortal shield.
Close on thy head thy helmet bright;
Balance thy sword against the fight;
See where an army, strong as fair,
With silken banners spreads the air;
Now, if thou be'st that thing divine
In this day's combat let it shine:
And show that nature wants an art
To conquer one resolvèd heart.

PLEASURE.

Welcome the creation's guest,
Lord of earth, and Heaven's heir,
Lay aside that warlike crest,
And of Nature's banquet share,
Where the souls of fruits and flowers
Stand prepared to heighten yours.

SOUL.

I sup above, and cannot stay
To bait so long upon the way.

PLEASURE.

On these downy pillows lie,
Whose soft plumes will thither fly,
Or these roses, strewed so plain,
Lest one leaf thy side should strain.

SOUL.

My gentler rest is on a thought,
Conscious of doing what I ought.

PLEASURE.

If thou be'st with perfumes pleased,
Such as oft the gods appeased,
Thou in fragrant clouds shalt show
Like another god below.

SOUL.

A soul that knows not to presume,
Is heaven's and its own perfume.

PLEASURE.

Everything does seem to vie,
Which should first attract thine eye:
But since none deserves that grace,
In this crystal view thy face.

SOUL.

When the Creator's skill is prized,
The rest is all but earth disguised.

PLEASURE.

Hark how music then prepares
For thy stay these charming airs,
Which the posting winds recall,
And suspend the river's fall.

SOUL.

Had I but any time to lose,
On this I would it all dispose.
Cease, tempter. None can chain a mind
Whom this sweet cordage cannot bind.

CHORUS.

Earth cannot show so brave a sight
As when a single soul does fence
The batteries of alluring sense,
And heaven views it with delight.
    Then persevere; for still new charges sound:
    And if thou overcom'st thou shalt be crowned.

PLEASURE.

All this fair, and cost, and sweet,
    Which scatteringly doth shine,
Shall within one Beauty meet,
    And she be only thine.

SOUL.

If things of sight such heavens be,
What heavens are those we cannot see!

PLEASURE.

Wheresoe'er thy foot shall go,
    The minted gold shall lie;
Till thou purchase all below,
    And want new worlds to buy.

SOUL.

Wer't not a price, who'd value gold?
And that's worth nought that can be sold.

PLEASURE.

Wilt thou all the glory have
    That war or peace command?
Half the world shall be thy slave,
    The other half thy friend.

SOUL.

What friends, if to myself untrue?
What slaves, unless I captive you?

PLEASURE.

Thou shalt know each hidden cause,
And see the future time:
Try what depth the centre draws,
And then to heaven climb.

SOUL.

None thither mounts by the degree
Of knowledge, but humility.

CHORUS.

Triumph, triumph, victorious soul;
The world has not one pleasure more;
The rest does lie beyond the pole,
And is thy everlasting store.

LONGLEAT HOUSE.

THOMAS KEN.

(Bishop of Bath and Wells.)

BORN A.D. 1637; DIED A.D. 1710.

THE well-known author of the Morning and Evening Hymns was born at Berkhampstead in 1637, and educated at Winchester School, whence, in due course, he passed to New College, Oxford, and returned to Winchester, as Fellow, in 1666. There he was appointed chaplain to the Bishop, and to a prebendal stall in the Cathedral. He distinguished himself in these offices by his devotion and zeal as a preacher of the Gospel. In 1679, he was made chaplain to the Princess of Orange, and went to Holland, where, by his boldness in reproving vice, he offended her husband (afterwards William III.). He in consequence resigned his office, and returned to England. In 1684, he became chaplain to Charles II., and showed equal boldness in his resistance to the profligacy of the court. The king, however, respected and honoured his consistency, and appointed him to the bishopric of Bath and Wells. Charles died before Ken entered upon his office, but he was, after some delay, confirmed in the appointment by James II. After the defeat of the Duke of Monmouth's rebellion, Ken visited and prayed with numbers of the unfortunate prisoners, and devoted much of his income to the relief of their wants; but so high was his character, that the Government does not seem to have looked upon him with any suspicion in consequence. It is well known how, afterwards, he resisted the king by his opposition to the reading of the illegal Declaration of Indulgence, and how, with the six other bishops, he was imprisoned, tried, and acquitted. Yet, at the Revolution, he was equally firm in refusing to take the oath of allegiance to William, and was, in consequence, deprived of his see. He lived in retirement and poverty till 1703, when Queen Anne conferred on him a pension of £200 a-year. He died at Longleat, where he had principally resided since his deprivation, and where most of his poems were composed.

The whole of his eventful life bears testimony to the Christian integrity and conscientiousness of his character. Four times we find him in a remarkable manner in conflict with the princes and kings at whose courts he held such conspicuous positions. In each case he was ready to sacrifice all rather than act against his conscience. And though he so boldly opposed them he still commanded their respect. Many Christians will strongly dissent from some of the opinions which he held so firmly, but all will admire his sincerity, and in his poetry will see the root of his high character in the ardent personal love to the Saviour which breathes forth in almost every line.

CHRISTIAN COURAGE.

STAND but your ground, your ghostly foes will fly ;
Hell trembles at a heaven-directed eye.
Choose rather to defend than to assail ;
Self-confidence will in the conflict fail.
When you are challenged, you may dangers meet.
True courage is a fixed, not sudden heat,
Is always humble, lives in self-distrust,
And will itself into no danger thrust.
Devote yourself to God, and you will find
God fights the battles of a will resigned.
Love Jesus ; love will no base fear endure ;
Love Jesus ; and of conquest rest secure.

GOD'S PROMISES.

My gracious God, Thy bounty I adore
Who hast enriched me with a plenteous store :
No monarch in the world, who ever reigned,
Such treasure had, which never can be drained ;
Not Solomon, with all his heaps of gold
And silver, which in streets as pebbles rolled,
Could with that wealth unlimited compare,
Which in Thy glorious promises I share ;
No pain, fear, want, temptation, danger, grief,
E'er seized me, but in them I found relief ;
My weakness strengthened, and my spirit cheered,
All tortures gentle made, and death endeared :
Thou, all-sufficient to all human need,
Hast aids proportioned for all states decreed.

PRAYER.

To offer prayer I never durst presume,
Did not dear Jesu's name my prayer perfume ;
'Tis, O my God, for the loved Jesu's sake,
That day by day address to Thee I make ;
That sinful, I dare Thee my Father own,
With humble confidence approach Thy throne.
O wondrous love, which gives us free recourse
To drink our fill at love's unbounded source,
Our sorrow to unbosom, and our need,
And a rich promise for each want to plead ;

With heaven while here below to keep commerce,
Familiarly with Godhead to converse ;
To intercede for blessings on mankind,
The pleasure of a charitable mind ;
To beg all graces, deprecate all bane,
Heaven for ourselves and others to obtain,
Strong consolations, and Almighty aid,
And wisdom, plots infernal to evade.

GOD IS LOVE.

By various names we Thy perfections call,
But pure, unfathom'd love exhausts them all.
By love all things were made and are sustain'd,
Love, all things to allure man's love, ordain'd ;
Love, vengeance from laps'd human race suspends ;
Love, our salvation, when provok'd, intends ;
Love, Lord, Thy infinite perfections join'd
Into all forms of love, to save mankind,—
Enlightening wisdom, and supporting might,
Grace to forgive, compassion to invite,
Thy bounty, in rewards which thought exceed,
Munificence, to promise all we need,
Truth, to perform, paternal, tender care,
A patient mildness, long to wait, and spare,
A justice, to chastise love's hateful foes,
Jealousy, curs'd rivals to oppose,
Benignity, to hear a sinner's cry,
Unbounded All-sufficience, to supply ;
They all are Love, love only is their aim :
My verse shall love and hymn Thee by that name.

THE PORTRAIT OF A MINISTER.

GIVE me a priest who, at judicious age
And duly call'd, in Priesthood shall engage,
With dispositions natural and acquir'd,
With strong propensions for the function fir'd ;
Whom God by opportunity invites
To consecrate himself to sacred rites ;
Who still keeps Jesus in his heart and head,
And strives in steps of our Arch-priest to tread,
Who can himself and all the world deny,
Lives pilgrim here, but denizen on high ;
Whose business is, like Jesu's, to save souls,
And with all ghostly miseries condoles.

Give me the priest these graces shall possess,
Of an ambassador the just address:
A father's tenderness, a shepherd's care,
A leader's courage, which the cross can bear,
A ruler's awe, a watchman's wakeful eye,
A pilot's skill, the helm in storms to ply,
A fisher's patience, and a labourer's toil,
A guide's dexterity to disembroil,
A prophet's inspiration from above,
A teacher's knowledge, and a Saviour's love.

Give me the priest, a light upon a hill,
Whose rays his whole circumference can fill ;
In God's own word and sacred learning vers'd,
Deep in the study of the heart immers'd ;
Who in sick souls can the disease descry,
And wisely fit restoratives apply ;

"A TEACHER'S KNOWLEDGE AND A SAVIOUR'S LOVE."

To beatific pastures leads his sheep,
Watchful from hellish wolves his fold to keep ;
Who seeks not a convenience, but a cure,
Would rather souls, than his own gain, ensure.
Instructive in his visits and converse,
Strives everywhere salvation to disperse ;
Of a mild, humble, and obliging heart,
Who with his all, will to the needy part ;
Distrustful of himself, in God confides,
Daily himself, among his flock, divides.
Of virtue uniform, and cheerful air,
Fix'd meditation, and incessant prayer,
Affections mortified, well guided zeal,
Of saving truth the relish wont to feel ;
Whose province, heaven, all his endeavours shares,
Who mixes with no secular affairs,
Oft on his pastoral accounts reflects ;
By holiness, not riches, gains respects ;
Who is all that he would have others be,
From wilful sin, though not from frailty free.

JESUS PRESENT.

WHEN our redemption was complete,
Thou, Jesus, didst to heaven retreat,
   And on the throne Divine,
   Make up the Godhead Trine :
There heaven Thy glorious body shall retain,
Till Thou at Judgment shalt the world arraign.

Yet with Thy saints ,'tis Thy delight
To stay, converse, and to unite;
    The Church in humble prayers,
    Thy gracious presence shares :
Thou at our hearts, when they are closed, dost knock,
And, entering, dwell, if we the door unlock.

How Thou, who wilt not heaven forsake,
Canst in my heart Thy mansion make,
    Is by experience taught,
    Though it transcends my thought.
I feel Thee knock : my heart, fly open wide !
Enter, dear Jesus, and with me abide.

Glory to Jesus, at God's right
Enthroned in majestatic light,
    Yet to converse art prone
    With saints below alone !
Live, Lord, with me, and when Thou wilt return,
Take my soul with Thee, and my dust inurn.

A SINNER CONVERTED.

I HAD only one thing to do,
Yet would a thousand things pursue ;
God only could exhaust my mind,
In God alone I rest could find ;
Yet o'er the world wild flights I took,
While I myself and God forsook.

My thought things perishable fill'd,
My soul, what was my poison will'd,
I fondly loved what I should hate,
Desired what horror should create ;
I lying vanities believed,
And trusted most, where most deceived.

God, shining on me from His throne,
Benignly brake this heart of stone.
All love to God, whose gracious stroke
Enflamed my heart, as well as broke !
Conscience, whom I with opiates ply'd,
Now wake, and be my watchful guide !

On Thee, my God, my thought shall muse,
Thee, sovereignly, my will shall choose,
My love shall to Thy love aspire,
The sole desirable desire ;
Thou wilt have all my heart or none,
The world I, for Thy sake, disown.

My soul shall long for blissful sight,
Shall in the source of joy delight ;
In hymns I, day by day, will sing
The favours of my heavenly King ;
My powers from Thee, my God, descend,
And shall to Thy sole glory tend.

Lord, I, self-offer'd, am not mine,
Keep safe this heart entirely Thine,
Let not hell-powers in triumph say,
That what was Thine they made their prey ;
Maim'd is the offering, yet sincere,
Heaven will its imperfections clear.

GOD A FATHER.

'Tis, Lord, Thy will that all mankind
Should love Thee with heart, soul, and mind ;
    And of all laws sublime,
    Love noblest is, and prime ;
But oh! by whom shall we be taught
To love Thy goodness as we ought?

Lord, 'tis Thyself, who hast impressed,
In native light on human breast,
    That their Creator all
    Mankind should Father call ;
A Father's love all mortals know,
And the love filial which they owe.

My Father! Oh that name is sweet ;
To sinners mourning in retreat,
    God's heart paternal yearns,
    When He a change discerns ;
He to His favour them restores,
He heals their most inveterate sores.

When pangs of the new birth they feel,
He to their pardon sets His seal ;
    O Love! exceeding thought,
    Which our redemption wrought,
Which endless bliss for saints prepares,
To reign with his own Son, co-heirs.

Religious honour, humble awe,
Obedience to our Father's law,
   A lively, grateful sense
   Of tenderness immense,
Full trust on God's paternal cares,
Submission which chastisement bears ;

Grief, when His goodness we offend,
Zeal, to His likeness to ascend ;
   Will, from the world refined,
   To His sole will resigned ;
These graces in God's children shine,
Reflections of the love Divine.

My love my tears can never rise
To a just filial sacrifice ;
   But Jesus for me bled,
   Both love, and tears He shed ;
For His love, tears, oh me forgive,
That I, Thy child, may ever live.

O Spirit of adoption ! spread
Thy wings enamouring o'er my head ;
   O filial love immense !
   Raise me to love intense ;
O Father ! source of love Divine,
My powers to love and hymn incline.

While God my Father I revere,
Nor all hell's powers, nor death I fear ;

I am my Father's care,
His succours present are;
All comes from my loved Father's will,
And that sweet name intends no ill.

God's Son, His soul, when life He closed,
In His dear Father's hands reposed;
I'll, when my last I breathe,
My soul to God bequeath;
And panting for the joys on high,
Invoking love paternal, die.

www.ingramcontent.com/pod-product-compliance
Lightning Source LLC
Chambersburg PA
CBHW031812230426

43669CB00009B/1117